Patanjali organizes his system of yoga as eight limbs. The first two of these eight limbs are called yama and niyama. They are universal principles of how to modify our behaviour and cultivate mental attitudes that lead to greater peace, contentment, and spiritual insight.

Because yama and niyama are the most approachable, they are sometimes considered only the beginning of the yogic path. But I believe they are both the beginning and the end of our spiritual life. I believe it is a mistake to think that the other six limbs of yoga take us to a place beyond yama and niyama.

Our spiritual life begins with trying to be better people, to cause less pain and to experience more peace. The heights of our spiritual life, whatever they may be, will only be an amplification of these basic goals.

Whatever its spiritual claims, no matter how impressive its history and tradition, if the teachings of yoga are not made practical, they are of no use to us. Rachel Bonkink has written a book that makes yoga practical.

I hope many students of yoga read and put into practice her excellent presentation of yama and niyama.

Paul Grilley
Ashland, Oregon
April, 2020

My dear friend Rachel has made it her mission to provide a fresh interpretation of the ancient yogic wisdom and to make it relatable to our modern-day world. Written with a mix of humour, vulnerability, personal experience and extensive study, this inspiring book will guide and support readers on their path towards a more authentic and meaningful life.

Carole Dieltiëns

To translate the ancient yoga philosophy teachings and make them accessible for everyone is no easy task. In this book, Rachel has done a fine job in making these concepts and ideas relevant, offering a practical and easy to understand application for integrating them into daily life.

I have had the pleasure of working alongside Rachel many times over a number of years, and have observed how she weaves the philosophy of yoga into her workshops and classes in a very down to earth and inclusive way. Highly recommended reading for yoga students and teachers or indeed anyone interested in deeper self reflection.

Hayley North, Yoga & Movement Teacher/Holistic Chef and founder of Holistic Kitchen Academy

Rachel's new book is not about yoga as we know it. It's about stretching your mind and becoming more fully yourself, the person you were meant to be. She has written an outstanding treatise that lovingly, kindly, and humorously introduces us to the 10 yogic principles to help us be more fulfilled and happy.

As a psychologist, this book makes my heart sing! Thanks, Rachel, for sharing your joy with the world.

Jennifer Wisdom, PhD MPH, Author of Millennials' Guide to Work *and* Millennials' Guide to Management and Leadership

I feel 'respect' for those who, by repetition, master their craft down to the finest detail.

I 'bow' for those who, in daily life, align mastery with the Divine.

How do you sit on your yoga mat?

In her own unique and candid way, Rachel created a book on how to flex your mind. This book is feisty, thought provoking, humorous and has tremendous depth at the same time.

Rachel guides you through ten powerful and challenging yoga principles. These principles will profoundly change your Being; on the mat, in your daily life and in your world.

At home or at work, we can all learn from this astonishing book!

Riet Lenaerts, Corporate Shaman, Shaman-Shape-Teacher

Rachel has translated universal and deeply human wisdom into clear guidelines. It's compelling and instructive at the same time. A must read in these confusing times.

Yamila Idrissi, founder of Kahwa Agency and Riad Feinek in Marrakech

FLEX YOUR MIND

10 powerful Yoga principles for less stress in a busy world

Rachel Bonkink

First published in Great Britain by Practical Inspiration Publishing, 2020

ISBN   9781788601795   (print)
       9781788601788   (epub)
       9781788601771   (mobi)

 Practical Inspiration
PUBLISHING

CONTENTS

PREFACE

What is Yoga philosophy? Most people have no idea what to imagine when they hear the term. In this book, I will give you a glimpse of it, in a down-to-earth approach, staying away from anything boring or too spiritual.

My inspiration comes from Patanjali, an Indian sage, and his ideas on ten principles that he describes in his book the *Yoga Sutras*. These ten principles are just a tiny aspect of the Yoga philosophy. It's my intention to spark some interest in you for the topic, to plant a seed that leads you to perhaps dive deeper after reading this book, and to share the teachings that I'm so passionate about in the best way I can.

The word Yoga can mean many things. In this particular context, Yoga describes a specific state of mind, a state where there is a certain kind of stillness and a limitation to the fluctuations of the mind.

Flex Your Mind is an invitation to explore Patanjali's ten principles with me and to realize that Yoga can be practised physically, and mentally, on and off the mat.

Giving well over 100 Yoga philosophy workshops made me realize that it was time to write down what I teach. There were some books out there but people didn't seem to resonate with them. Most of my clients are either in corporate or are self-employed and many don't seem to have a particular interest in going through Sanskrit, ancient scriptures and all kinds of new terminology. However, the interest to learn about creating more peace of mind in a hectic world is definitely there.

At the same time, the Yoga teachers that joined my retreats seemed to struggle with passing on the knowledge in a way that didn't scare their students away.

And that's exactly where my own struggle began: how could I respect and honour the tradition, while at the same time making this knowledge light and accessible? Leaving out the ancient languages of Sanskrit and Pali was a conscious choice – explaining them in-depth in one version, kicking all the terminology out again in the next version of this book, and happily repeating this scenario twice, up until my niece, with a bundle of love, bluntly told me that she loved what I was saying but that she completely lost the plot and all interest every time I started mumbling those Indian words. She believed that I knew what I was talking about but it would be nice if I could keep it a bit 'real'; life is complicated enough already as it is.

I instantly knew what to do. I made a glossary at the end and I'm forever grateful to Katinka for her valuable input as so many people have told me that they struggle with the terminology in Yoga philosophy and Buddhism.

I shared what I felt and sensed was necessary and enjoyed writing about my previous working life as an operational director and stressed-out workaholic – a time when things were, let's say, 'different' in every single aspect of my life.

The invitation is there to just start reading. I'm convinced that these ten principles will help you change unwanted behaviour, get you to worry less and help you find a way to flex that beautiful mind of yours to find some more peace of mind.

ACKNOWLEDGEMENTS

I want to thank my mom for being my biggest fan, always there for me, always promoting my work and ready to listen. I feel blessed and proud for having you as my mom.

Thanking my friend Alice Morrison, whose own display of self-discipline in writing her books has encouraged me to finish mine, to push through and get it out there. Without her, I might still be wondering what should go in and what shouldn't, instead of actually writing.

A very special thanks goes to Carole Dieltiëns, Hayley North, Jennifer Wisdom, Riet Lenaerts and Yamila Idrissi who have provided me with incredibly valuable feedback and the confidence that what I wrote made sense.

My worldwide coaching clients and Yoga students gave me the opportunity to learn and grow and it has been an honour to coach and teach every single one of them. The input they have given me, from the cover design to actual content selection, has greatly influenced and shaped this book.

This book would not have been possible without the help of professionals. Thanks to Teresa Antunes, who was the first person to ever have a look at my draft, as well as a big thanks to Dan Shutt for editing the next versions.

The work behind a book with a quality look and feel to it is immense. I am beyond grateful for choosing the well-oiled machine of Practical Inspiration Publishing for making this book with a special thanks to Alison, Shell and Judith.

And my eternal gratitude to Paul Grilley for his review and endorsement; his teachings made a profound impact on the way that I teach Yoga.

ABOUT THE AUTHOR

Rachel Bonkink is no ordinary Yoga teacher. She holds a master's degree in Commercial Sciences and has had a long corporate career as an operational director. She has studied Traditional Chinese Medicine and has been a life coach for over ten years.

She specializes in organizing and hosting the most amazing Yoga retreats, from Costa Rica to Scotland, from France to Morocco, leading groups, teaching Yoga and meditation in stunning locations and inspiring people to embed the principles of Yoga into their everyday lives.

From the very start of her own Yoga journey, the philosophy of Yoga resonated with her more than any individual *asana* or posture. She has continued to read, study and train to deepen her knowledge of Yoga and meditation.

Between retreats she lives in rural Morocco, where she can be found by the beach writing, studying and enjoying life, doing the things that she loves the most.

INTRODUCTION

Leaving ancient texts like the *Mahabharata*, the *Upanishads*, the *Vedas* and the *Hatha Pradipika* nicely where they are in history, as they are outside the scope of this book, I pick up with Patanjali, an intellectual and ascetic who lived in ancient India around 200 BCE. He put together what was then known about Yoga and made it into a systematic approach to investigate the nature of the mind, writing down 195 threads of wisdom where he explains the nature of Yoga. Today we refer to them as the *Yoga Sutras*.

This is my free-spirited interpretation of some of these threads of wisdom. The interesting thing about working with ancient texts is that you could have ten different teachers explaining the theory of Patanjali in ten different ways, and they could all be 'right'.

Patanjali is the author of the *Yoga Sutras*, but much more important are the commentaries added to actually understand it all, as the *Sutras* themselves are almost impossible to read.

So what is this Yoga philosophy all about? The *Yoga Sutras* can be seen as a roadmap to find a peaceful state of mind. Patanjali describes this roadmap as 'the eight limbs of Yoga'. In this book, I focus on the first and second limb of this system, *yama* and *niyama*.

Asana, the practice of Yoga postures, is the third limb in this Yoga path, and this is where most modern Yoga students are introduced to Yoga. Breath control and deepening levels of concentration and meditation make up limbs four through to eight.

Yama and *niyama*, limbs one and two of the eightfold Yoga path and the focus of this book, concern ten principles that, when integrated into your own practice, will bring you more peace of mind and an easier way to deal with the challenges of modern life.

These principles go way beyond being an ethical code like the Ten Commandments and there is nothing religious in the way that I will elaborate on these principles in this book. When we truly live these principles, we are able to return to our core Being. The way we are in our purest form. This means that we will want to live by these principles, without requiring extra willpower to continue practising them; once we really understand the true meaning of these principles, we will want to live our lives according to them.

These principles are not about what we cannot do; there is no judgement when we succeed or fail; there is no 'Principle Police' and there is no punishment. We should rather see the principles as suggestions to start exploring our own actions and our thinking patterns. In fact, they are so much more about what we can do and about who we really are than about what we should refrain from doing.

With full respect to tradition, I took the liberty of leaving out as much Sanskrit as possible – an ancient language from India in which the *Yoga Sutras* are written. I wanted the principles to resonate as much as possible with Western mindsets. I minimize the cultural differences, as I believe this knowledge needs to be passed on. The same for the Pali language, in which the Buddha shared his message. In each chapter, I have added small bits of concepts and ideas from both Buddhism and the *Yoga Sutras* as they complement each other on several aspects, in order to understand and calm our minds.

While teaching on retreats and workshops over the years, I have found that so many people are interested in knowing more about this *stuff* but very few people are interested in reading an entire book about 'Yoga Principles and Philosophy', especially when it's full of words that we don't really know the meaning of.

I'm taking a leap of faith here, as some might find that I cut the philosophy short, whereas my only intention is to pass on the knowledge to as many people as possible.

I'm passionate about bringing these principles into our daily lives, as it has changed just about everything for the better in my own life. This book is a way to get you interested and also inspired. Maybe even inspired enough to dig a little deeper.

This book focuses on the very base of what we now consider as Yoga in modern Western societies. And that is why I chose to use a capital 'Y' in the word 'Yoga', as Yoga in this sense can mean so much more than only the postures.

Exploring *yama* and *niyama* can seriously deepen your practice, boost your meditation and give you more insight into the nature of your mind. These teachings will not be dogmatic or oppressive; on the contrary, with little breakout boxes for reflection and exercises at the end of each chapter, my intention is to lighten things up. I call these tasks 'change-makers' as, for sure, they have the potential to change your life for the better.

To be able to read this book, there is no need whatsoever to have practised Yoga or meditation, nor to have any intention to start with any of that. Anyone with an interest in having more peace of mind can find inspiration in this book.

My ambition and intention with this book is for you to have a really nice read – something you will want to re-read. It is not a theoretical or an accurate book for scholars. It's more of an introduction to what Yoga philosophy can mean to you in your daily life, how you can start being more comfortable with your own Being and showing the real 'you' to the world.

Translating the text, making it workable – that is what all advocates of this philosophy have been doing from the start with the threads of wisdom. Yoga is a living tradition, something to practise on a mat, but above all *off the mat.*

I have to thank all the students and clients over the years, well over 1,000 by now, as without them this book would not have happened. I am so grateful for the many discussions, for the inspiration, insights and the many stories that were shared on retreats, workshops and coaching sessions. I am deeply grateful to have been able to study with many great teachers, but the greatest teachers have been my students and coaching clients.

Looking forward being a spiritual friend to you.

1

NON-VIOLENCE

The first principle we will explore is non-violence. All other principles have their origin in *ahimsa*, the Sanskrit word for non-violence. Non-violence equals universal love. It means completely abstaining from causing any kind of pain or harm to any living creature, either by thoughts, words or deeds.

This is easier said than done. The way we approach non-violence goes beyond the 'Thou Shalt Not Kill' of the Ten Commandments. When we address non-violence in Yoga philosophy, our intention is different. It goes way beyond something *we may not do* and stretches into something we want to cultivate and nurture.

Violence can mean many things. There can be violence in the way you close a door, for example, or in the way you talk to a stranger, or simply in the way you enter a room. There's violent energy when you are angry with your kids or when you wish for unpleasant things to happen to someone who cuts you off in traffic. When you're constantly criticizing yourself, never feeling content with your own accomplishments, as subtle as they may be, these judgemental thoughts can truly be violent.

Of course, some violence is much more obvious. I grew up in an overtly violent environment. My family went through several traumatic events and as a child I was exposed to a world that no child even needs to know exists. It was not until I started studying the Yoga philosophy in more depth that I came to realize exactly how violent my upbringing had actually been. Today, I work very hard to limit any violence occurring in my life, even in the subtle realm, because now I understand that the overt violence I experienced as a child isn't the only type of violence that exists.

In this chapter, we are going to look at how violence manifests itself in our daily lives, what we can do practically to cope with it and how to bring in more kindness, for the benefit of ourselves and others (in that order).

It is a challenge to practise non-violence, as we seem to be surrounded by violence in our daily lives. And, unfortunately, running off to an *ashram*, or spiritual centre, somewhere in the Indian countryside will not free you from encountering violence. Been there, done that. There, you might encounter deadly scorpions, buzzing bugs, and you might find *ashrams* packed with irritating group members or bossy teachers. And how about stepping on an ant or 'killing' vegetable life for supper?

These kinds of examples can encourage you to become aware of the breadth of the type of violence – and non-violence – I'm talking about. As you deepen into this concept, you may find that at a certain point, you even begin asking yourself on a daily basis how you can display the most non-violent behaviour in any given situation.

Let's zoom in first on some forms of violence we come across in our daily lives.

Practising active kindness

Intention of the day – I will be nice to every Being I meet today

How utterly cool would it be if everyone on the planet had this intention today? To restrain from anything that is violent to oneself and others.

Overt violence

The act of war is one of the ultimate manifestations of violence. In 2018, there were still over ten active conflicts worldwide, from African Somalia to Asian Myanmar. It's hard to grasp that with all of our human history, intelligence and in the quest for world peace, we still manage to have people in distress, fear and horror in so many countries.

It may seem like there is little we can do. But I assure you that refusing to close our eyes to what goes on in our world, acknowledging these facts and helping in any way we can will actually work to counterbalance this kind of violence.

War is the most overt type of physical violence, but physical violence is what most people tend to think of when 'violence' is brought up. In that context, we tend to think mostly about the violence that is being done to others. However, things become really interesting when we think about the violence we demonstrate towards ourselves – on the Yoga mat, for example.

Can Yoga be violent?

As a teacher, it's fairly easy to spot the student who does not practise non-violence in a Yoga class. Instead of looking peaceful, their bodies and especially their faces usually start to tense up, and their breathing becomes jagged. It looks far from 'peace in action'.

Non-violence on the Yoga mat is all about becoming aware of our appropriate edges without pushing ourselves beyond a point that might cause us harm – that might be violent. It's about getting stronger and more flexible and, while pursuing these goals, knowing exactly when we are hurting ourselves and when we are staying within our own safe limits.

I strongly encourage people to go to Yoga classes, to Pilates or to work out and exercise. By doing so, we can train ourselves in becoming more aware of the things that may be causing us harm. And this helps us out in our day-to-day situations. More often than not, we do not have time to sit and evaluate, let alone meditate on it. A decision as to whether or not we need to take action is made in a split second.

When we train our bodies and minds, non-violence can become a reflex. This way, we automatically become aware of our instinctive reactions and choose the most non-violent action.

There is a non-violent action for nearly any given situation. If we feel that someone insults us, for example, our initial reaction might be to defend ourselves. A trained mind will assess the situation and, if there is no danger, the choice might be to not defend ourselves, but rather to respond with compassion to the one lashing out.

This is also true in a Yoga class, when a posture is given that you know is tricky for your knee that has been operated on, for example. Your initial reaction might be to just push through the pain and try to ignore it, because you don't want to give up. A strong and trained mind will be fully aware of the pinching feeling in the knee and hold back a little, or even come out of the pose entirely, completely ignoring what everyone else is doing in class and focusing fully on what causes harm and what is violent to the body. Coming out of a pose because of a sharp pain is never a sign of weakness; on the contrary, there is zero gain when there is any sharp pain in Yoga.

Ethically speaking, 'cause no pain' holds the crux of the yogic teachings. This means to cause no pain to other Beings, and especially to cause no pain to the self.

Does this mean we should do lame practices and mostly lie on our backs and relax? Not at all! We can have a vigorous practice, making our body and mind stronger, as long as we practise with loving kindness and consciousness about what our body can and cannot do at a particular moment.

When I see people struggling in class, I suggest that there is probably a very good reason for their struggle. They might carry some extra kilos because they haven't prioritized a healthy diet. Maybe they aren't as strong as they used to be because all their time went into work, parenting or caregiving.

In the ancient scriptures about Yoga, there was no mention whatsoever of when a posture was perfect, aligned or advanced; simply knowing this sometimes helps as well. The only thing that was said about postures in the ancient scriptures is that they should be comfortable, steady and done with a relaxed mind. The postural Yoga we see today is purely a modern invention.

Verbal violence

Next to physical violence towards oneself or others, examining how verbal violence manifests in our lives can also be eye-opening in our journey towards increased joy and happiness. Verbal violence relates to the things we say to each other. Cursing, swearing, bad language, gossip, complaining, raising our voice – all this can go under the label of 'verbal violence'.

It took me a very long time to stop using the F-word. At some point, it seemed like we all really needed the F-word in our company, to add some sort of power to our words. The more stressed we became, the more we swore. However, when I stopped swearing or using bad language completely, the tone and depth of my conversations changed. I began noticing that most people around me also stopped swearing.

Do you swear? Do your friends swear? How do the people that you spend most time with talk? Is it positive or rather negative? Is there a lot of complaining going on around you?

Sometimes, just noticing these things can give us an insight into our own energy levels. It is not hard to see that negative talk, whether it's coming from ourselves or coming from the mouths of those around us, will not lift us up or give us more energy. This awareness is key, because verbal violence can be hidden in the smallest of things.

Quite often, one of the very first questions that we ask when we meet new people is 'what do you do for a living?' It's an easy question to ask, and it's usually a perfect antidote to awkward silent situations. However, it can also be a very violent question if the person you talk to is in a job that is socially considered as lower on the status ladder, for example. Or higher. And what if this person has just involuntarily lost his or her job?

There is another aspect of this question that can make it violent if we're not just asking the question out of general human interest. Sometimes this question can be a tool to control and oversee the situation, or a way to assess and judge the other person. Our subconscious mind could go something like this: *Aha, you're a 30-something banker in the city, meaning you are ruthless, make a ton of money and only think about yourself and your career.* Or it could say, *Oh, you're a 44-year-old paediatric cardiologist, so this means you're a wonderful person who really cares about people and wouldn't hurt a fly.* It's so easy to judge people based on this question alone. But who is the person behind the title?

There is even a third reason why we might need to revise the way we ask our questions. After our curiosity about a person's job, our next question is often probing about someone's marital status, followed by asking whether or not they have kids.

Have you ever wondered when you just randomly ask this question – because that's what we do – how somebody feels who has just lost either their partner or a child? How this person might not even yet know how to answer your question? They might not have figured out yet whether they are still married, or if they now have two or will always have three children?

There is nothing wrong with asking questions, of course. We just need to be aware of how they will impact others, as well as being aware of our own motives for asking them. Bearing this in mind, we can choose to be more careful with the language we use, in order to cause the least amount of harm.

The next time you meet someone, it might be more than enough to simply ask how the person is doing and really listen to the answer, giving the answer your full attention.

Violence through judgement

I recently spent Friday evening at a friend's house in Belgium and together we watched the talent show 'The Voice'. More than the show itself, I was struck by the avalanche of critique I heard from my friends about what the participants were wearing and how they looked. It would have been so easy for me to just go along and join in, but it was also wonderful to not participate. Why? Because I have full respect for the people who put themselves out there. As far as I'm concerned, one candidate may be more gifted and/or skilled than another in terms of their voice, but that is it. The competition was meant to be about the voice and nothing else.

My friends didn't notice, but I was quite amused by simply observing them. They had just finished a stressful workweek, the kids were finally in bed, and now there was time to finally chill. What could be easier and more relaxing than spending an evening criticizing others?

Being a Yoga teacher or a life-long practitioner doesn't free you from a judging mind – especially nowadays, when everyone seems to have an opinion on how Yoga could or should be done, and what it actually is. This book is no different.

We may critique and give voice to what we don't agree with. The main idea, however, when referring back to non-violence, is about how we communicate when we don't agree with something. Can we snap out from our own disturbance of wanting to be right the whole time? To so desperately wanting to tell our own stories? Can we be conscious of our actions and think before we act, to check if something is harmful or compassionate?

Only then will we understand what Gandhi was trying to convey when he said, 'Let us be the change that we want to see in this world'. We can protest, we can disagree, but we can do so in a compassionate and non-violent way. Violence in whatever form is not the answer.

The truth is that when we are violent, when we lash out at someone, we are not in balance. On the contrary, we have lost our natural calm, harmony and serenity. Practising non-violence is not something we try to do;

it is something that we *are*. When we see the essence of ourselves in others, the only way is to be gentle, compassionate and full of love towards all sentient Beings. When non-violence becomes a lifestyle, we will start to feel it in all aspects of our lives.

When I moved to Morocco, I had a chance to see this judgement in myself. For one thing, the concept of standing in line in Morocco is very simple: one does not. When you apply European queuing rules, you might need to spend the night at some places because it will never be your turn. Four years ago, I judged Moroccans to be ignorant, disrespectful and unmannered. Now, I realize that this is the way things work here. It has nothing to do with respect. You just go with the flow and the guys at the local little grocery shops, or *hanouts*, are masters in multitasking and helping multiple customers at the same time.

Every single day in this country has been a learning experience for me. This simple example has taught me that non-queuing is a cultural difference, but neither way is objectively better than the other.

Nowadays, I check in with myself to see whether I have all the possible elements and knowledge to judge a particular situation *before* I judge it. So far, I never have!

Nama-stay

Internal work feeds the external choices we make. Do you dare to sit down for a minute or two and just sit? Without paying any particular attention to the breath or anything else, just sit and check in with what is in your mind right now, allowing whatever is there to be there: feelings, emotions, desires. It can be so intriguing to observe your own mind. Have the courage to sit and stay; nama-stay.

Violence in thought

Next, let's talk about subtle violence against ourselves; more particularly, we are going to zoom in on our thoughts. General consensus among several studies comes to the conclusion that we have about 20,000 to 50,000 thoughts per day. That's a lot of thoughts.

The question is: how many of those thoughts are non-violent towards ourselves and others? Almost everyone that I have asked this question has smiled and then frowned. We can really be our own worst enemy with all of these thoughts about ourselves.

How do you get up in the morning, and what happens when you look in the mirror? Does your inner critic immediately blast off a spur of negativity – about failing to go to bed early, once again, or a nice little rage about not looking the age you once looked? Too thin, too fat, wrinkles, pimples, eye bags, grey hair, no hair etc.

The words we say to ourselves – would we vent them out loud to a five-year-old? No, the child would be traumatized for life! So, why do we say them to ourselves repeatedly? That is pure violence.

As we will see later on in this chapter, being aware that we have these violent thoughts towards ourselves holds the very key to change. The same goes for worried thoughts. When we become aware of our worries, we can start to change the pattern.

Many people master the Art of Worrying. They worry about their health, their kids, their jobs, pandemics, war, poverty; they lie awake at night, not being able to shut off their worried thoughts.

Worrying is usually very violent. We are experts in packaging worry as something more acceptable, such as caring, problem-solving or creativity, but it mostly comes down to running multiple disastrous *what-if* scenarios.

Acceptance

A way to get over negative and violent thoughts is to accept things as they are. Acceptance can be a huge hurdle as it is often misunderstood. We may wonder, *Shouldn't I be 'further' already on my spiritual path? Will I ever be truly happy, free and content?* This constant search for perfection maintains pressure on us to be better, perform better, look better, even meditate better. *Do your best, be the best* – 'the winner takes it all', as the song says. At school, at university, at sports. Most of us have been taught that we need to be different to and better than everyone else.

At the same time, while on our quest to be the best, we are also desperately looking for union and increased connection with others. We long to belong, and dwell in the feeling when we think we don't. These two thoughts are a solid foundation for confusion and negative thinking patterns.

I love Carl Rogers' paradox: 'When I accept myself just as I am, then I can change.' In this vein, I ask you: do you fully accept yourself, right here and right now, with all your flaws and imperfections? When we find acceptance for ourselves as a starting point, we leave a lot less room for negative thoughts to come buzzing in.

We will address the concept of acceptance in more depth in Chapter 7, which covers contentment. However, there is a strong link between non-violence and contentment, because violence is often a symptom of how discontent we are. We can change by starting with acceptance. Putting more effort into your diet, for example, could be beneficial for your body – but can you accept your body right now, without a single negative or violent thought about it? Can you embrace every single part of it, knowing that it has brought you this far already?

Darkness cannot drive out darkness; only light can do that. Hate cannot drive out hate; only love can do that.

Martin Luther King, Jr.

Connection fail: lack of respect

In every chapter you will see the title 'connection fail' popping up. As the Sanskrit term Yoga is most frequently interpreted as 'union', I will examine how not living by the principles gives us a connection fail with ourselves and the world around us. There are more options to translate the word Yoga, but in this book we will keep to this translation of union, binding together, connection.

If we want more union, it's impossible to bring violence to anyone or anything. In a way, we are all one. The good thing is that we don't need to acquire any extra goodness or compassion. We just need to remove the habits and blockages that hide them.

I was blessed with a 13-year relationship early in my life. By ending it, I realized who I had become. We met right after high school and had the best of times, but slowly we grew apart and became very different people with conflicting aspirations. I wanted to conquer the world, to travel and reach the top of the corporate ladder, and he was totally ready to settle and slow down. We already had the house, the cars and the cats, so he was on the winning end.

The best description of myself at this time would have been: *a bitchy 30-something C-level who thinks she is going to rule the world with her BMW, Cartier watches, business-class trips and fancy function title.* I now realize that I was so self-obsessed that there was simply no room for me to respect my partner any more.

To not respect someone – anyone – is always a red flag. If you are unable to respect a person, you need to stop for a minute and reflect. It is in giving respect that you will receive respect back and that negative thoughts will disappear.

If respecting a person that has caused you harm is too much for you right now, you might consider letting go of the negative feelings that you hold towards that person. At least you can take steps in that direction. If you would normally vent your feelings about this person verbally, you can try not to speak about them out loud for a while, for example. By doing so, less energy is given to your negative feelings, which might make them less acute.

Respect, compassion and forgiveness... but not passivity

True non-violence is about respecting all life and rising above anger, hatred, aggression, fear, jealousy, resentment, envy and attachment.

But non-violence is surely not something passive!

In the *Vedas*, a collection of scriptures dating back to 1,500 BCE, we find a story about a *sadhu*, or wandering monk, who would make a yearly circuit to a number of villages. One day as he entered a village, he saw a large and menacing snake. The snake was terrorizing the villagers and making their lives difficult. The *sadhu* spoke to the snake and taught him about non-violence; it was a lesson that the snake heard and took to heart. The following year, when the *sadhu* made his annual visit to the village, he again saw the snake. How changed he was. This once-magnificent snake was now skinny and bruised. The *sadhu* asked the snake what had happened to cause such a change in his appearance. The snake replied that he had taken the teaching of non-violence to heart and had realized the error of his ways. Thus, he had stopped terrorizing the village. Because he was no longer menacing, the children now threw rocks at him and taunted him. He could hardly hunt and was afraid of leaving his hiding place. The *sadhu* shook his head wisely and said that while he had indeed taught the importance of practising non-violence, he had never told the snake not to hiss.

This story shows us that non-violence doesn't mean passivity. Neither does non-violence mean that you agree with everything. Personally, I can say that I am more passionate than I ever was in my busy corporate days, but I now work in a gentler way, with full respect for other people's opinions and values and far less attention to my own ego and its urge to be right.

Regardless of non-violence, we have to face the challenges of our planet and respond to our governments, for example, to show them that we disagree with certain decisions and policies. We do this without being violent, and at the same time without becoming lethargic or dwelling in some misguided spirituality that tells us it will all work out and everything is meant to be.

Non-violence towards animals

We do not think of ourselves as part of the animal kingdom – not conceptually, and for sure not practically.

Physical violence towards animals is often a touchy topic and there is no one-size-fits-all prescription here. However, the ancient text of Patanjali leaves literally no room for interpretation. 'If you see the *atman* (God) and suffering in every Being, you will keep a strict vegetarian diet out of compassion.' This is without exception, and this would be non-negotiable with Patanjali.

Mahatma Gandhi said that a nation and its moral progress can be judged by the way it treats its animals. We can't deny that our Western factory farming is mostly harmful and violent. With all kinds of undercover videos from farms and slaughterhouses available, it's impossible for any of us to say that we are not aware of the horror that goes on in our meat industry.

In some climates, though, people might need animal protein because there is nothing else to eat. This is very different from the choice to eat meat that comes out of the harmful meat and fish industries.

For those of us who have the option, it's important to ask: where does our meat come from? Was it a happy cow up until it landed on our plate? How did it live and how was it slaughtered? Was there any harm and violence to the animal and our planet?

I'm very aware that it can be a bit of a minefield to actually know what is good and not good for the environment – let alone to figure out what is 'healthy' these days. Keep reading, learning, experimenting, feeling and using your common sense. Local produce might be more interesting than produce that has travelled across the globe to end up in your supermarket. A couple of days without meat per week might be a good idea once you start researching the link between cattle farms and our global water supplies. Since the main idea of this chapter concerns how to bring non-violence into all aspects of your life, to embrace it as a way of life to feel balanced and lighter, diet may be a great place to start.

Holding peace

My own journey with non-violence has focused on not going overboard with my work – an old and ingrained pattern for me. The ambition and passion that I feel are brilliant and they push me forward, but ambition is still also one of my major pitfalls. In fact, I used to do back-to-back week-long Yoga retreats. It made sense, as I didn't need to fly anywhere else, the logistics were easy and I got really familiar with the places. But I wasn't checking in with my own needs. I have since learned to rest and retreat myself after hosting a retreat for others.

When choosing to speak out or not, *holding my peace* is probably one of the most noticeable actions that have changed over the years. I've heard the idea of 'choosing your battles', but I consider that a rather violent way to put it; instead, I ask myself this question: *would my comment make anyone happier?*

If I disagree with someone, I will probably mention that I don't agree but I might choose to not defend my opinion if I see that the other person would love to be right. For me, it's not worth it any more.

And that's just it – going forward, you'll have to figure out what it's worth to you. Do you want to inflict violence? Upon others? Upon yourself? How and where are you willing to incorporate non-violence into your own life?

Hostility

As a text without commentary, the *Yoga Sutras* are very vague about the exact meaning of the principles, but what Patanjali did point out to us were the results of 'living the principles'. The text mentions literally that the person who becomes firmly grounded in non-violence will experience that other people who come near will naturally lose any feelings of hostility. This means that when we put non-violence into practice, this naturally brings harmony and inner peace, which in turn results in other Beings feeling no violent emotions or aggression towards us.

We will end this chapter with the words of Gandhi, a global icon of non-violence, who illustrates the fine link to our next principle and chapter on truthfulness; for Gandhi, the two are scarcely distinguishable.

> Non-violence and truth are so intertwined, it is practically impossible to disentangle and separate them. They are like the two sides of a coin, or rather of a smooth unstamped metallic disc. Who can say which is the face, and which is the reverse?

And yet Gandhi maintained the distinction.

> Nevertheless, non-violence is the means; truth is the end. Means, to be the means, must always be within our reach, and so non-violence is our supreme duty.

Change-maker: compassion

The next time someone lashes out at you or is rude to you for no obvious reason, ask yourself: *what could be going on with this person that caused them to behave in this manner?* Make no mistake, someone who is completely happy and at peace with him or herself doesn't lash out at other people. Take a moment to wonder: *was I my friendliest self to this person? Was I respectful? Could there be a cultural difference involved? Could it have nothing to do with me at all?* See if you really need to defend yourself. If you do, go for it. If you don't, see if you have it in you to offer some compassion. Then just watch what happens!

Change-maker: two non-violent minutes

This only requires two minutes of your time. How about trying to not have a single violent thought for two minutes?

See if you can only let peaceful thoughts enter into your mind. If we are truly seeking peace and non-violence, we have to step out of our judgemental behaviour and train our minds. You can do this at any given moment. On a terrace, with lots of people passing by, would be an excellent place to practise.

2

TRUTHFULNESS

Our next concept is truthfulness, etymologically derived from the Sanskrit word *satya*.

For our modern minds, Sanskrit can be a difficult language to understand; it doesn't allow us to translate words one by one as Sanskrit is an intrinsically vibrational language. The concept of *exploring* Sanskrit terms is much more accurate than the belief that we are *translating* a language used thousands of years ago.

When we look at the word *satya*, many scholars agree on *sat* meaning 'true essence', 'true nature', that which is true, or even 'to be; being'. It is therefore commonly translated as 'truthfulness'.

Throughout this chapter, we will discover that the concept of *satya* is very layered, and it is much more complex than the difference between telling the truth and lying. What this principle teaches us is to go (back) to a state of mind that arises when we operate from our pure nature, our pure consciousness, our truth, our Being. It may not come to you as a surprise that love and relationships get a lot of attention in this chapter.

When touching on the principle of truthfulness in workshops or on my Yoga retreats, it triggers quite a lot of people. They don't want to be thought of as liars, nor as harming others with their words or actions, and most people will answer that they are truthful and honest.

Here are some of the questions that might also trigger you as you're reading this book.

- How honest are you?
- Who gets to see the real you?
- What was your last lie?
- What is it that you really need, right now?

We will start our exploration of the principle of truthfulness by addressing these questions in just a little bit more detail.

How honest are you?

Is being honest the same thing as being truthful? Are you not honest when you tell a lie?

Are you not truthful when you are dishonest? Of course, you don't lie. We were taught from a very young age that we must not lie, so we feel ashamed if we have to admit to people that we are not so honest about the truth.

When you work in sales, you might hear yourself saying that you have loads of experience in a certain kind of project when in reality you have only done similar things, and nothing that big. Back in the day, I heard myself saying all of these things – and more than once!

Is it being dishonest if you really do believe, like I did, that you will be able to deliver the project? Isn't twisting the truth in order to reach a certain goal just showing your passion and ambition? After all, you might not make the deal if you are 'too honest'. Right?

How about this one: do you instantly need to tell your partner that you *might* feel something for someone else? At what point are you being dishonest? At what point do you cross marital or relationship boundaries?

Or this one: every time you meet a life-long friend, the one you've known since college or even longer than that, you feel afterwards like you've been run over by a truck. You can't place your finger on it exactly but you have no energy left after meeting this person. Will you tell them what's really going on the next time they ask to meet?

Or my favourite one: 'let's not tell grandma; it's not good for her heart to know. She'll worry too much. It's better that she doesn't know.'

So, the whole family will collectively lie to her.

Who gets to see the real you?

One way to define truthfulness is *being truthful* – the act of being honest with yourself and not cheating others for your own gain or to discredit them. This means that your thoughts, words and actions are aligned with who you really are. You are being the real You.

You might think, 'Am I not always myself?' Well, yes, but consider how we can wear different versions of ourselves at work, at home, with friends, with family.

You change to meet the needs of the situation, but when you live in truthfulness you can be the same person at work as you are at home. There might be a slight professional difference, but it's hardly noticeable.

I lead lots of Yoga retreats and workshops every year and my friends and even my mom will attend many of these – they are an easy way for my friends to see me and for us to spend some quality time together. I have to act truthfully around them on retreat just like I would at home. Trying to fake it when my mom is around is not a good idea. Lots of people are so surprised with this situation, telling me that they could never ever have their mom around in a working situation. They admit that they can become a very different person in very different situations – there's even a different look for different situations. Switching between all those identities requires a tremendous amount of energy, so why not just be you? What is holding you back from not being your true Self, from not living as the imperfect, perfect person that you are?

I would consider someone telling you that 'with you, what you see is what you get' one of the best compliments you can ever receive. Embrace it fully!

If you want to be the best version of yourself, why would you even think about lying to someone? It's not because you can't; it's because you don't want to. Throughout this chapter and this book, it will become quite clear that the ten principles of Yoga philosophy are there to assist you in becoming who you truly (already!) are. And being truthful is a crucial principle in attaining just that.

When discussing truthfulness, though, it is of utmost importance to remember that the principles have a specific order. Non-violence is not the first principle by accident. Non-violence is the foundation of all yogic philosophy; doing no harm to anyone should always be at the top of your mind.

This means that the *brutal truth* might not be the best option to share with everyone. Some situations ask for non-telling when the truth might be hurtful, so omission is the best non-violent solution. But before we resort to this as an easy way around speaking our truth, we need to become conscious about our choices.

I have a question for you…

Imagine your friend has asked you, 'Does my butt look fat in these pants?' If you believe the answer is 'yes', try responding with, 'Maybe a different model would suit you better'. This way, they might not buy this style again. Or maybe they don't care what you say after all.

There was a question, and you answered it in the kindest way, telling your truth. It was your opinion, and it was asked for. When not asked, do not give your opinion – not about pants, not about asses, not about anything.

What was your last lie?

Do you really dare say it out loud? To whom did you lie, and why? Do you dare write it down? How does it make you feel?

From hiding an affair to that little text message *explaining* why you're late, research has shown that the average adult lies about ten times a day. We all lie, but not all lies are the same.

We lie to protect or promote ourselves, to impact or manipulate others, to avoid the discomfort of telling the truth – and sometimes we don't really know why we lie. You might come up with a few of the following reasons.

- I don't want to hurt their feelings. They can't handle the truth. I can do without the drama when they find out.
- What will they think of me when they find out the truth about me?
- It's not really lying; it's just bending the truth a little.

If any of these thoughts sound familiar, you have been lying.

I could explain every single one of these thoughts to you, but in all fairness there is no real need for it. We all recognize when we are tempted to lie, but when we give it a second thought we might find that there is no real need for it.

Connection fail: liar

One of the definitions of Yoga is 'union', which is ultimately what we all strive for – more connection with ourselves, more union with the people we love, with the people we work with and maybe even with strangers. As mentioned before, we will zoom in on this connection failure in every chapter, as connecting with others is such a wonderful thing to do. However, at the same time, these days it seems so difficult to achieve for so many.

When we lie, we accomplish the exact opposite of union. One lie leads to another and we separate ourselves from others instead of finding ways to naturally bond.

And, perhaps even more importantly: the more we lie, the more disconnected from ourselves we become. Most people don't realize that lying to others actually has a massive impact on themselves – a negative impact, because negative energy is shared with others. Why is it that lying feels bad after a while? It's even in our language: we need to 'come clean' about something.

How to stop lying?

Step one is to become aware of your lies.

During my corporate days, I would eat out at restaurants about five times a week – Japanese, Italian or whatever fancy new thing had opened up in town. Cooking was a no-no; healthy food was unknown territory.

In those days, when we were a party of three, I would make sure to book a table for four just to get a decent spot. I didn't want to end up in the corner at a little table for two with an extra chair. On entering the restaurant, the waiter would ask where our number four was, which was of course logical. At that time, my answer was also logical: number four was ill or couldn't make it. No big deal; I didn't even think about it as lying. In retrospect, it most certainly was lying.

Why is this a big deal?

Because it makes no sense whatsoever to lie to another human Being. What you are creating is an ease of lying. You become completely unaware of it. It can even become a habit.

Lying comes with a risk, though. If there's one thing that I have learned, it is that 'what comes to you, always matches you' (thank you Abraham and Esther Hicks) – so you shouldn't be surprised if later the waiter is not 100% honest about when exactly some of the things he serves were made.

Remember: what you give is what you will receive, in some form or another, 1,000-fold.

Ok, so how do I handle the situation with the party of three now? It's quite simple. When I book, I ask for a nice table that fits three people comfortably, instead of a table for two with an extra chair. Same story, very different energy – and no need to lie.

Do you find yourself in situations where your initial reaction is to come up with a lie? Before starting off with a lie, quickly check if you can be honest. What are you afraid of? Is that something you can bring to the table or not? What is holding you back?

Maybe there are also doubts across the table from you, of whatever kind. It is so often the case that by addressing the issue we can solve the problem, instead of making it worse – as, without a doubt, one lie will lead to more lies.

Telling the truth will probably save you time, energy, effort and maybe even money.

Really?

Having worked all those years in a corporate environment, I have heard an immense variety of excuses for why people were late, didn't deliver, didn't show up, did something they shouldn't have etc.

What have I found out? *The greater the explanation, the less truth there was in it.* So, don't be silly when making excuses. Maybe your boss or clients have been around long enough to come to the same conclusion as I have.

What is it that you need right here and now?

Might it be more coffee, a partner, a break-up, a hug, peace of mind, love, sex, wine, a holiday, sun?

There might be desires, cravings or longings popping up and there's absolutely nothing wrong with that. As long as we don't get consumed and ruled by these desires and cravings, it's only human to have them.

Cultivating truthfulness means that we start asking ourselves: *why do we give a specific answer?* If you need more coffee, is it just a habit that you have, or does it reveal something else? Does it reflect the fact that you are more tired than you can even imagine or admit to yourself? Would you dare to go a step further and explore why you are so tired? What (or who) is taking all that energy from you?

What stops you from jumping for joy out of bed in the morning? What excites you? What's behind it and can you be honest about it? What is holding you back, or what are you afraid of?

No fear

If non-violence will lead us to a situation of absence of hostility, the practice of truthfulness will lead us to a state of fearlessness. This is what Patanjali tells us is the result of truthfulness.

When you are fearless, you are always able to speak your truth. People know that you always speak your truth and that there is no need to fear you, in the sense that you will not lie about anything.

You are not afraid of what people think of you, nor are you afraid of how they will react or cope with the / your truth.

This makes sense, as a person who is purified and who will do no harm need not be feared. At the same time, this person will feel no fear, as the thought of being violent to another Being has left their mind. How wonderful would it be to have no fear of losing our job, our possessions, our loved ones, our reputation, our life?

The Four Noble Truths

Over the years, Buddhism has given me so many insights on why I do the things that I do, so I happily bring some of its aspects into this book.

One of the core principles of Buddhism concerns the Four Noble Truths, which apply to what we're discussing here.

The First Noble Truth is the fact that we, as human Beings, suffer. Because we are embodied, we constantly feel the need to run towards pleasure or away from pain. Thinking that we can find lasting pleasure and avoid pain is what in Buddhism is called *samsara*, a hopeless cycle that goes round and round endlessly and causes us to suffer greatly.

Our cravings are revealed as the reason why we suffer in the Second Noble Truth. Luckily, there is a cure for all this suffering in the eightfold path, which is explained in the Third and Fourth Noble Truths.

The eightfold path is often represented by the Dharma wheel. Each spoke of the wheel represents an element of the path. These are right vision, intention, speech, action, livelihood, effort, concentration and mindfulness.

The two spokes of right intention and right speech refer to the idea that we actively need to cultivate the truth, to speak our truth and be aware of it. This side path is an introduction to Buddhism; I will come back to it every now and then in the book to show you that many of the great philosophies guide us towards the same ideas.

The secrets that hold you

Both in my private life and in my life-coaching work, I have come across a lot of people who tell me their secrets. Secrets that they haven't told anybody else. During our sessions, I'm not expected to act on the secrets they tell me, but the fact they are able to share with someone they trust can relieve so much of the burden they carry.

Secrets are blocked energies and you can be quite sure that they will stick, one way or another, somewhere in the body, the heart and/or the mind. Just telling a story to someone you trust can bring immense relief. If you don't talk about it, it will not just go away. We are all familiar with the concept of 'the elephant in the room'.

Secrets can become like prisons, as keeping secrets takes so much energy. It feeds shame and at a certain point the secret holds you instead of the other way around. So please find someone you trust and tell them whatever secret you have that burdens you.

If there's nobody you can trust with the secret, you can always get in touch with me. If you're reading this book, I'm happy to connect in real life and be there for you.

Principle Police

Is *not telling the truth* considered to be lying? This is an often-asked question when we discuss truthfulness, and it's an interesting question as there is no Principle Police to judge and punish if you're doing it right or wrong.

When it's a lie, you will probably feel it. When something is not entirely aligned in your body and mind, and you don't feel well about not telling something, it could have the same meaning as lying.

This whole journey is about becoming more aware so that we can come closer to our true Self. We can ask ourselves what Patanjali, the author of the Yoga principles, meant and just this little notion will reveal an incredible window of opportunity to grow in every single situation where we have doubts. We can take the responsibility to grow, to be conscious and aware of our own choices. We become empowered as we gain control. We can choose our words and reactions wisely – or not.

Silence is golden

Silence can teach you the value of your words and the value of your speech.

When you go on a silent retreat for one, three, five, ten, 100 days or even longer, you become aware of how much you talk to yourself. There's usually so much mental chatter that many people suffer serious headaches just from listening to it all in the first few days. (The cold-turkey coffee withdrawal doesn't help either, but that's a different story.)

The silence allows you to examine this chatter. And this will eventually guide you in your outward conversations as well. If you become aware of your thoughts, you can work with them, direct them, and this will highly influence your interactions with other people and yourself.

Lying to ourselves

We all have these great resolutions and ideas on how we are going to make our lives even better. *Yes, I'm absolutely convinced, after this retreat I will meditate every day. On Monday, I will start my diet. I will work less and spend more time with my family. The gym will be my go-to at least three times a week from now on. I will not look at my phone first thing in the morning.*

The thing is, when we come up with these master-plan ideas for raising the bar of our lives, we can sometimes already hear that little voice in the back of our minds saying: *No, you won't... you can't follow through with anything, so why would you even think you will this time? It's been on your list for so long, what changed? Just forget it, it's not gonna happen.* Does this little voice sound familiar? Sometimes it's not so little – it's more like someone yelling and screaming in your ear.

We all have this voice. The reason why some people succeed and some people keep making new resolutions and plans is that the ones who succeed don't give too much airtime to the voice. Better yet, in an ideal world, they don't even listen to the voice. And the reason why they can ignore the voice is because they have a reason for doing what they are planning to do. And that reason is so strong that they will go through with their plans, they will follow through, even when they don't feel like it. It's like they are being pulled towards their goals. But, in order for that to happen, one needs to be very clear and thus very honest about the goal.

If you're very honest, for example, why do you want to meditate? I will take this example as so many people struggle with continuing with a regular practice. Perhaps your reason is something like: *They say it's supposed to be good for you...* If that's the case, then please save yourself the trouble; this is not going to get you 'to the cushion' (an expression that is often used in meditation) when you don't feel like it.

Your reasons need to be crystal-clear, and they have to be strong enough to push you forward. This aspect of goal-setting will come back several times in this book, as it's a key element in attaining a happier state of mind. For now, just reflect on *why* – when you set up certain goals that perhaps you have been setting up for years, why do you usually fail on the execution?

Out goes the joy

It takes about seven years to become a good acupuncturist or to know a thing or two about Traditional Chinese Medicine, so I will be careful with the shortcuts that I'm taking when I refer to the topic in this book. I'm sharing it here as, especially regarding truthfulness, it explains so beautifully how everything in our body, mind and spirit is connected.

In Traditional Chinese Medicine, every organ has a function – or, better yet, a responsibility. Before we continue, it's crucial to know that this doesn't relate to anything on a physical level, rather on an energetic and spiritual level.

With relevance to our topic of truthfulness, there's a saying that 'the tongue is the root of the heart'. This means that any kind of problem with speech or not telling your truth could be caused by, or could cause, imbalances in the heart's energy.

Shen, which can be translated as spirit, consciousness, mental wellbeing or mental vitality, lives in the heart, where it retires to sleep at night. If our *shen* is disturbed, our sleep may also be disturbed – along with our heart energy.

The emotion of the heart is joy. When we experience joy, we are feeding our hearts. When we lie, our *shen* is disturbed, our hearts are disturbed and it is so much harder to experience true joy. We are numbed and might get an overall feeling of *urgh…* and boredom. We might try extreme sports or put ourselves in extreme situations, to at least feel 'something'.

If we are speaking our truth, from our heart, only good things can come to us because we are then resonating with the ultimate truth. We cultivate and feel joy, even when there's nothing tangible or obvious to be 'joyful' about. We are aligning ourselves with the person we want to become.

I love you

Being ignored by the person we want attention from is such a painful experience. I have been there (never a pleasant experience)… What I have found out, the hard way, is that when we look deep enough and really examine what is going on, we realize that the person who does not love us is ourselves.

When we crave attention from others, we're often in a state of dependence and insecurity and could use some more self-love. Self-neglect and a low sense of self-worth are usually the things that push us to such a needy stage. And, in essence, that person was just the final step towards a big wake-up call. What we need to do when we feel longing for someone, or even start to obsess over them, is to first start loving ourselves again.

Sit down, breathe, relax and think about this for a second. This also counts when you are in a relationship that is not going so well. Could the above be true and make a little bit of sense? Can you be uncomfortable for a minute and realize that what I just mentioned could potentially be true and happening with you right now?

If you have something to say to someone you love, whatever it is, and you feel you need to express it, just do it – if your intention is pure. If it's not in any way your intention to make the other person feel bad, tell them. When you're in love with a person and there's even the slightest chance that the other person might feel the same about you, tell them. Don't wait. There's never a right moment anyway. Life is short; you do not want to regret or ponder about a love that might have been.

What is the absolute worst thing that can happen? That the feeling is not mutual. So what? The other person can feel honoured and strengthened in their ego because someone fell in love with them, and you can move on.

Not telling is a choice, of course, but when it becomes a burden, it will take a lot of energy from you to stick around or hang out with this person. And that is not being authentic or truthful – neither to yourself nor to the other person.

I have known all along, my love...

If you have been lying to people that you love, it might be that they already know, on some level. Don't underestimate the energy that you send out and never underestimate the sensitivity that some people have. Maybe they knew all along and by lying you were the one suffering the most...

Should we always come clean, in everything? I don't think so. Every single situation is different and there's no point in generalizing. What I do know is that we *feel* when speaking our truth is our best option. To be able to feel this, we need to connect deeply with ourselves and cultivate love and kindness to ourselves before we can do anything else.

When you bring non-violence and truthfulness together, then you might find the ultimate cocktail to success on the path to more peace of mind and joy.

These two principles, brought into practice together, will lead you to surprising results. You can stop reading here and these two principles will still keep you busy for at least one lifetime – even without the other eight principles we have yet to discover! In the next chapter we will see how the principle of non-stealing can make an impact in our modern lives.

Change-maker: Big Brother is watching

How do you actively cultivate truthfulness? By finding those areas in your life where you can speak more truth. Where can you be more honest? If you already consider yourself to be quite honest, how can you be even more honest – to yourself and to others?

Who are you when nobody is watching – when you're 100% sure that nobody can see or hear you? It's a very simple question to ask yourself. What's your diet like? What do you watch? How do you vote?

Change-maker: analyze your day

How often do you go through your days on autopilot? You get up, you go through the motions of your life and at the end of the day you feel exhausted and overwhelmed, as though you didn't accomplish anything. *Ugh...*

Your time goes to where your priorities are.

Writing down everything you do in a day is one of the best ways to get a grip on your time consumption. Only then can you see and analyze if you are doing the things that produce the outcomes you desire, or if you are wasting time.

To do this exercise, get a pen and paper and write down everything you did yesterday. Include things such as brushing your teeth, making the bed, having breakfast, spending time on social media, details about what you did at work etc. The order does not have to be chronological – just get it down on paper. This will give you an accurate idea of what your days actually look like, and whether you can be truly honest about it.

Change-maker: the Buddha says...

The following are sayings from the Buddha, from *A Dhammapada for Contemplation*, a contemporary rendering of the ancient text by Bhikkhu Munindo. Simply read them and feel them resonate.

82
On hearing true teachings,
the hearts of those who are receptive,
become serene like a lake,
deep, clear and still.

202
There is no fire like lust,
no distress like hatred,
no pain like the burden of attachment,
no joy like the peace of liberation.

258
Those who speak much
are not necessarily possessed of wisdom.
The wise can be seen
to be at peace with life
and free from all enmity and fear.

3

NON-STEALING

If we see non-violence as active kindness and non-lying as the act of being as honest a person as we can be, then non-stealing, our third principle to zoom in on, can be translated as being as generous as we can possibly be.

The Sanskrit word for non-stealing is *asteya*, derived from the root word *steya*, which means 'to steal' or 'to rob'. By adding the prefix 'a' it becomes *asteya*, or non-stealing.

On the surface, non-stealing seems to be quite straightforward. *Don't take what's not yours*, right? I assume that most people who read this book do not compulsively steal items from stores and so on, so focusing on the non-physical realm is much more interesting. Here's what stealing can look like in this context.

- When you are late, you are stealing the other person's time.
- When you are checking private emails during your boss's time, you are stealing the company's work capacity.
- When you dominate a discussion, you are stealing the opportunity for the other person to express their opinion.

- When you don't mention the creator, you steal the idea.
- When you are busy with your phone instead of listening to someone, you are stealing quality time from the both of you.

We will zoom in on these and other examples to further explore the idea of stealing, which might turn out not to be as simple as you expect – especially when we consider how we can steal from ourselves.

Because you are beyond greed

The definition of non-stealing leaves hardly any room for interpretation; it means to abstain from taking things that are not yours.

Beyond the physical, we can steal another's time, joy, energy… And, with our current behaviour, we may also be stealing from future generations when it comes to our environment and natural resources. We can even steal from ourselves.

Let's explore how non-stealing might pop up in daily life and what can be done about it.

'I'm so sorry that I'm late!' When you are late, you steal time from the one waiting for you, as this person could have done something else in the meantime or could have spent some more time in another activity before meeting you.

Being late is a violent affair, as the first thing that you have to do when you arrive late is to excuse yourself. Greeting without needing to apologize first will feel a lot better – especially if you don't have to begin by convincing the waiting party that your being late has nothing to do with your eagerness to see them.

You could have the most brilliant excuse, but your excuses could make the situation even more violent. Some people are experts in reverse psychology when they are late. 'I'm late because I couldn't choose which flowers to pick because you are so special and I spent too long in the flower shop. How can you be upset? Don't you like the flowers? It took me over an hour to choose them, and you can only focus on me being late? How rude! After everything I do for you. Maybe we shouldn't be meeting at all?'

These kinds of situations can leave the one waiting completely flabbergasted. What the heck just happened? They are one hour late to our date and I'm the one feeling bad? However one flips or manipulates the situation, or however incredibly beautiful the flowers are, the fact is that time was stolen from the person waiting.

How cool would it be if the person you are supposed to meet would show up an hour before you actually arranged to meet up? You don't see them; they wait somewhere very close by, not bored, amusing themselves. They have no problem whatsoever with being early; on the contrary, they just wanted to make absolutely sure that they would be on time, to spend as much time as possible with you. Not taking any chances with traffic or other unexpected things. Just because they value your time together so much. Tell me, just how cool would that be – if someone felt that way about seeing you, being together with you?

What our timing might tell us

If you are the kind of person who's usually on time but for a specific event you notice that you are running seriously late, check in with yourself. It could be pure coincidence, or something else could be going on under the surface. Do you really want to go and see this person? Is there something holding you back, making you late?

Bringing the Yoga philosophy into everyday life means bringing in more awareness about our thoughts and our behaviour. Grabbing these little moments to check in with ourselves instead of going through the motions is what makes us more conscious and aware.

Time is money

Watching videos or checking emails in your boss's time is stealing time from your boss. During this time, you could have worked for the benefit of the company. In some environments, it's completely acceptable to check personal emails and engage in activities that have absolutely nothing to do with your work. In many other environments and companies, we only do it when the boss is not looking, hiding our behaviour. Even when you are the boss, by behaving in this way you are stealing working time from yourself. You could work on something for your company; instead, you choose personal benefit.

Why do we do it? If we are an employee, we are getting paid to do a job. That job, whatever the job title is, is not to check private emails and watch videos for pure amusement.

I can remember some frustration on this exact topic from my very early days as an employee. Imagine this tiny little software-selling company, all very free and fun, with a big boss who's in London and nobody in charge in Belgium.

The non-existing-management idea was great for us, as long as we could deliver results. The boss would fly us to the UK, where we attended the Royal Ascot races and had our company meetings in Windsor, at the most posh place you can imagine. It was so cool, and I am so grateful that I had the opportunity to experience all of it. After a while, though, we no longer delivered the expected results. In fact, there were no results at all as the entire market was spiralling down at a pace faster than any of the Ascot horses could ever run. And in an absolutely normal reaction, the first thing our boss did to increase results again was to start checking up on just about everything. Working hours were checked, all of a sudden we had to be on time, emails were checked, the number of cold calls had to increase, we were entitled to fewer breaks etc. I need not explain how upset we felt, as there was no clear communication about what was accepted and what was not, leaving a lot of grey zones. I felt so underappreciated and frustrated when one day I got a comment about checking a personal email – I was looking for another job – but had no mention of answering a work-related email at 10pm the day before because of some kind of emergency.

We need to be crystal-clear on the rules about things like this, so that we do not steal anybody's time or hurt people's feelings. If you don't know the rules in your current work environment, I can only encourage you to ask about them to prevent frustration – on all sides. It's so much easier when you have these things clear.

No, don't do that! I...

In most cases, when we give 'advice' to others, what we are really doing is stealing their enthusiasm or joy. Of course, we hush our egos really quickly by saying that it's in their best interest that they follow what we say, but is it really?

Imagine that you tell one of your friends that you are going on a Yoga retreat in Morocco. You might immediately receive a little rant about this person's own experiences in Morocco – how incredibly busy the big Jemaa el-Fnaa square in Marrakesh was; that they got lost in the *souks* (markets) of Fez and almost fainted in the Sahara Desert because of the heat. And, oh yes, they got that beautiful carpet in Tangier and camels are really smelly. 'You should do this, see that, make sure that you do not… and… and… and…' This is not very interesting if it's your first visit to Morocco, you're going on a Yoga retreat in Essaouira and are not going to visit any of the places they mentioned. It is even less interesting if, upon hearing the stories, your enthusiasm about going there starts to decrease. 'What made you choose Morocco and where are you going exactly?' could spark a very different conversation.

You can usually notice when you have stolen someone's joy if they stop elaborating on their story or if they get defensive – feeling the need to defend their choice.

Don't do what I did!

Very similar to the previous example of giving advice and stealing people's enthusiasm or joy is stealing people's experience, which refers to not allowing the other person to have their own personal learning curve.

Although we want to, we can't always prevent other people from making mistakes or making what in our opinion are the wrong choices – for starters, because this is simply our view on the situation, and our own idea of right and wrong. Furthermore, just because something didn't work out for us, we do not absolutely have to prevent others from trying the same. Maybe, just maybe, they need to go through an experience and learn from it, as we did.

As a life coach and mentor to both new and established Yoga teachers and lots of other entrepreneurs, I guide people who are setting up or expanding their business. My track record doesn't lie; I get results and I manifest whatever I want. *I know how that sounds, but it is true.* So, in this context, we agree that the coachees follow my advice and we get the results that we have envisioned together.

In my private life, I'm friends with lots of people who want to start their own business. This is a very different situation, as often they will tell me of their ambitious plans without asking for my advice. Listening to someone who might disapprove of their ambitious ideas is usually the last thing on their list, and I can see why; some just don't want to hear that their idea has some flaws.

I see a lot of them begin with no vision whatsoever, listening eagerly to their so-called six-figure business gurus. I get it; these supposedly super-successful teachers play exactly on all the negative feelings people have and show you their solution, which is to follow their courses. One may be even more expensive than the other but you will realize your dreams, just like they did.

Yes, there's a firm judgement in the latter but it hurts to see people spending money they don't have to follow courses they don't need. The thing is, as a friend, there is only so much that I can do when someone believes that they are following their dream and don't want to listen. When my advice is asked for, I always give my opinion and experiences, while stressing that these are my personal experiences. It could be very different for other people.

Energy vampires

Some people are real energy vampires, stealing your energy, and they may have no idea why. You could be one too. If you talk more than you listen, this could be a little hint that, for some people, you too might be an energy vampire. If you complain more than you feel grateful, this is also a clue.

Listening is not just 'not talking'. True listening means that you are allowing what someone else says to change you – without any judgement, without jumping to conclusions: simply listening to what the other person is telling you. Sometimes people just need to tell you something and there is no need whatsoever for you to solve their problem or share your opinion.

Hush!

On my Yoga and meditation retreats we often practise the art of listening. We pair up and for a period of three minutes, one person talks and the other person listens. After three minutes, they switch roles. The topic is not that important, as the idea is to not engage in any conversation. One person listens, and only listens – this means not being preoccupied with what they will say afterwards – and the other person talks.

An assignment that is not too complicated, you would think, but there are so many people who aren't able to listen without starting a conversation. They just have to talk and give their opinion. Which is perfectly normal! I had exactly the same reaction in the beginning! Most of us had a schooling system where sharing our opinion was seen as being smart. And we just continued trying to position ourselves as smart, bright, interesting and so on. By truly listening, though, we might be able to connect to other people on an entirely different level.

Years ago, Sarah Powers introduced me to these little chats, or *dyads*, and I can't recommend enough experimenting with the idea of true listening in workshops, trainings and, most of all, in your own daily life.

Why do we steal?

We all know that stealing is dishonest. How can we be enlightened (and I know that is a big word, so you can replace it with *being the best version of You*, if you like) when we take what is not ours? It makes no sense whatsoever!

So why do we steal? We can find inspiration and explanations in all great traditions, and while they use different names and terminologies, they usually reflect the same three to five reasons.

These reasons, or 'poisons' in Buddhism (*kleshas* in Sanskrit), are ignorance, ego, attachment, aversion and clinging to life. We usually see the effects of these root causes being displayed in our greed, anger, desire, delusion, envy and sloth. Let's zoom in on greed a little bit more, as one of the reasons we steal what is not ours. The other poisons are not discussed in depth as they are well-known words and concepts. This doesn't mean that there's nothing to elaborate on – they are crucial in Buddhist studies – they are just not in the scope of this book.

Greed

An economic system that puts all emphasis on money and the pursuit of personal gain has created a mentality of greed in all Western societies. We always tend to want more, especially more money, more wealth and more status. When is it ever enough? How many handbags do we really need? How many pairs of shoes do we need or how much money needs to be in the bank?

Or, diving in just a little bit deeper: what gap are we trying to fill with material stuff? What are the beliefs that make us think that we will not have enough? Desire and greed are interconnected, like so many of the other concepts are. The unhealthy desire of wanting more causes a tremendous amount of suffering in the Western world.

Need and greed

'There is enough for everyone's need, but not for everyone's greed.' Why not re-read this quote from Gandhi a couple of times and take a bit of time to reflect on it?

But it's not all negative – not at all. Lots of people in this world could surprise you as they are not driven by greed or any material gain. Some people have a very different perspective on wealth. Meet Mohamed, who has been driving me around Morocco for the past four years.

Every year, King Mohamed VI of Morocco visits Marrakesh. On a particular day, we happened to be around; I even walked past him in the medina without realizing at first what all the fuss was about.

The king is known for granting people's wishes on the spot, so I asked Mohamed what he would ask the king if they would ever meet. Money was not the first thing he mentioned. In fact, when I asked him about money he had to think really hard, and only after me insisting on a number did he say, '10,000 dirham would be nice'. That's about 1,000 US dollars.

I was so surprised and asked, 'Why ask for so little? This is one of the wealthiest men on earth! You could ask for anything!' I will never forget his answer: 'But I don't need more…'

Wanting more is so deeply engrained in most of our Western minds as this is what we are taught from a very young age: more is good, less is bad. Right there and then, this Yoga person just got a very wise lesson from the man who drives her around in Morocco. The concept of 'more, more, more' was still so much embedded in my being. *If I can get more, why not go for it?* It was the very thing that got me to quit my very well-paid job in corporate: realizing that it was never going to be enough for me, that I would always want more – more money, more status, as long as it was *more*. And here we were, years later, and Mohamed gave me a little reminder.

Lots can be said about the reasons and root causes for stealing. Entire psychology books have been written about it, and there are a million ways to examine it all. What I would love for you to develop is awareness. Awareness of when you steal, awareness of when you are not being You, as in the best version of You.

In what follows, I've listed a quick overview of all the 'poisons'. Just read and see if they resonate.

Ignorance

Ignorance in this context means that you don't even realize that you are stealing.

Ego

Usually, we perceive the ego as something rather negative. In the *Yoga Sutras*, however, ego is not only perceived as negative. Ego is described as a sense of self or personality. It comprises all the thoughts and reactions of a mind, shaped by experiences, preferences, habits and fantasies.

Our egos are there to protect us. They see danger and despair in every situation and it's their goal to keep us safe – whatever the definition of 'safe' might be in a given moment. When the ego identity is threatened, we react unconsciously to protect it.

Attachment

Remember the Four Noble Truths from Chapter 2? The main teachings of the Buddha? His message is that desire, attachment and clinging will bring us nothing but suffering. They will cause us to steal other people's joy, ideas and so on.

The root of attachment

In the old days they just loved their lists and rankings! The eight limbs of Yoga; the eightfold path of Buddhism; the ten principles, starting with the most important one of non-violence...

There's another one here, as Vachaspati Mishra adds in Bryant's book *The Yoga Sutras of Patanjali*:

'Ego is the root of attachment, just as ignorance is the root of ego: consequently, ego precedes attachment in the list of *klesas* as ignorance precedes ego.'

Aversion

We can feel such an aversion to being poor, for example, that we always want more and more, and we would do just about anything never to be poor. If the aversion is deep enough, we could even justify (for ourselves) taking things from others who, in our opinion, might have enough and can do with a bit less.

Immortality

Being 'the richest man in the graveyard'. We all know this expression, yet we still completely ignore it and do not live by the wisdom contained in these words.

Connection fail: taking what is not mine

By stealing we don't exactly honour the definition of Yoga that we are using in this book – 'union'. More connection with ourselves, more union with the people we love, with the people we work with and maybe even with strangers. When we steal from others, in a physical or non-physical way, we will attain the exact opposite and we will feel more disconnected from others. It becomes a mine-and-theirs affair. *I want what is yours.* When we're practising active kindness and honesty (the first principles), it's almost impossible to be so self-absorbed that we would take what is not ours. So, once again, we see here why non-violence is our very first principle.

Besides stealing from other people, let's have a look now at how we can steal from ourselves.

Stealing from yourself

Before we dive in, let me ask you a question: while you are reading, right here and now, are you still 'here'? The Buddha said: 'Be where you are... otherwise you will miss most of your life.'

When your attention is not where you are, you steal from yourself the experience of being alive in that moment. If you do that most of the time, you will miss your life. If, during your workout, you're thinking about what happened before or what might happen afterwards, you are stealing your own quality time. You are not there.

I see it so often when I go to one of my favourite lunch cafés in Essaouira. It has great salads and vegan stuff so it's usually quite busy with travelling foreigners. (There's a limit to the number of *tajines* [typical Moroccan dish/cooking pot] one can eat...) What strikes me is that most of them are on their phones or laptops, planning the next part of their trip – checking out the coolest places to stay, where to eat, reading up on the ten best things to do in the next city and so on, making sure they don't miss anything and that they can tick off all the highlights. Preparing all this takes up time, time that could have been spent truly enjoying and exploring the magic of this little town. Especially in a place like Essaouira, you need time to wander around, get lost in the narrow side streets, have tea with a spice man and run into all kinds of unexpectedness. There are no big museums and not too many spectacular things to visit; it's just a little town you need to experience. But for all of that to happen, you need to be very present and to fully enjoy the experience. What I see, however, is people being in a constant state of transit, in the process of going to the next thing, and the next, and the next.

Wake up!

We need to try to be awake every single moment, in every task, to avoid the autopilot state at all times. If tomorrow you have to make a big decision, this could be all you think about today. This means that you are preoccupied and don't really notice what you're eating or drinking. The decision is all you can think about – or so you think. As we know by now, we can direct our thoughts, as we make them. If you're only thinking about tomorrow, you have missed a memo here and there as you haven't understood what life is all about. Maybe there's no tomorrow. This is not dramatic. Not everyone who goes to bed in the evening wakes up the following morning. We take it for granted but it's not so obvious.

To make it slightly less drastic, you could get a simple food poisoning because you weren't paying attention to what you were eating, and there will be no decision to make tomorrow because you will be in the bathroom for most of the day...

This is exactly what happened to me on my first Toubkal experience. We were about to climb North Africa's highest mountain, with six retreat participants. The day before the retreat started, I was still busy. I had just finished a retreat in Portugal; there were still lots of little things to take care of, and I had a meal in the most mindless way – eating while at the same time sending emails and organizing stuff. It was only right after eating the quiche that I sensed something was very wrong. Instantly. I will spare you the details, but it involved toilets and a whole lot of willpower to make it to the top that year.

Thoughts

Change Your Thoughts – Change Your Life is the title of a great book by the late Wayne Dyer. Just the title is worth a moment of reflection. If we constantly choose to listen to violent thoughts, for example, we are stealing an opportunity from ourselves to have a moment filled with positive and loving thoughts.

As soon as you become more mindful of your thoughts, you have the choice to focus on whether the thoughts are useful or not. Do you continue worrying about finances or the environment, or do you actually get into action and start coming up with ideas on how to change the whole situation? Do you continue feeling ashamed or will you learn from what happened and create a new strategy for yourself, so you respond differently when something similar happens? What is important to realize is that we definitely have a choice, and there's no need for us to be continuously hijacked by our thoughts.

Browsing time away

Wasting time on social media, mindlessly browsing around from one post to another or from one series to another – by doing so you are taking away time from yourself that could have been spent in a different or more productive way.

Many people feel stress or pressure and don't know how to cope with ever-growing to-do lists, but when asked about popular series, they know all of them. So, apparently, there is time to watch these for hours on end. There is absolutely nothing wrong with entertainment or watching series, reading, amusing ourselves and so on – it's just interesting if you then 'run out of time'.

The million-dollar question

Do you dare to dream? By not daring to dream, we steal away the potential of our dreams. We risk potential growth because if we can't dream it, then for sure it will be a lot less likely to happen.

What if you received 1 million US dollars, right here and now? What would you do? Some people don't even want to answer that question; they don't even want to think about it, because they are convinced that it will never happen. OK, but what if? Do you dare to dream?

(I know someone in Belgium who received 1 million euros from a distant aunt; she didn't even know this woman personally. True story.) It can be so refreshing to have a think about what you would do next. I hear many people say that they would instantly quit their jobs, leave their partner or go on a holiday. My usual response is to ask if they really need 1 million dollars to proceed with those plans.

I remember vividly asking my mom this exact same question when we were having a juice, looking out over the Atlantic in Essaouira. She answered that she would love to do a three-week *panchakarma* (Ayurvedic cleansing programme) in Sri Lanka. She even knew exactly where to go as she had had the address written down for years. 'But mom, you don't need 1 million dollars to do that? It's not exactly cheap to fly to Sri Lanka from Europe but unless you are planning to buy a part of the hotel... Why would you need so much money to go there?' That same night, we made all the bookings and I got to spend three awesome weeks in Belgium, taking care of the cats and her little doggy. Leaving the cats and dog alone for three weeks was the last excuse holding her back in fulfilling a longtime dream.

My mom is not the only one holding back on dreams. Most of the time, we're just making up excuses to not follow our dreams. We might think we're not worth such an expense or experience.

Overall, a lack of money and time seem to be the perfect excuses to not grant ourselves opportunities. And that's exactly why I love asking the million-dollar question; it provides so much insight into some of the barriers and blocks that we have put up. And it can be as simple as gifting ourselves with a wonderful holiday.

The antidote: the art of giving

I have mentioned it before, but if there's one thing that I have learned on my yogic path, it is that whatever you give, it will come back to you tenfold. Whether it's something very positive or something negative, it will come back to you.

We give because we want to give. We do not give simply because we know something will come back. We give love, passion, inspiration and so on.

Have you ever noticed that when you feel good and go out, it seems as if everyone is having a good day and all you see are smiling faces? And when you are having a bad day, you only meet grumpy people everywhere and everything seems to go 'wrong'?

Giving instead of taking

Consider: are you giving more than you are taking – to and from the world, or in your relationships?

Bling-bling

It is stated in the *Yoga Sutras* that when we are firmly established in non-stealing, we are presented with all the jewels and treasures in the world. Jewels could even be in the literal sense as people will trust their belongings to someone they know will not steal from them.

When we look at it from a more spiritual and non-physical perspective, we see that there is no greed in a generous mind. You can't conceive taking something that isn't yours if your main aim is to give. When this is your aim, 'gifts' in all different meanings of the word will come your way. People will literally start giving you material gifts; the universe will give you silly little gifts like free parking spaces or extra seats in a plane. Embrace it all as the more you give to others, the more you will receive.

If you feel lonely, send a message to someone who you know is lonely. When you need a friend, be a friend. When you want to feel loved, send love to someone. Is it really that simple? Yes – and the best way for you to find out is to give it a try!

The principles are all interconnected

When we steal, not only are we being dishonest, which links back to the principle of truthfulness (Chapter 2), but there's violence involved as well, which we tackled in Chapter 1, as someone or something will suffer some kind of harm if you take what is not yours.

Not considering ethical norms or codes, but seeing this on a much larger scale, we remember what is truly important. Our next chapter focuses on another crucial aspect of our Being: energy! Without the right energy, it will be difficult to live up to our highest goals.

Change-maker: demonstrate what you value

I have been giving this assignment for years on my retreats and, as I read so many books, I honestly can't remember whom to credit for this one. It faded into the background but by reading Brendon Burchard's book *High Performance Habits* I was reminded of the idea and I tweaked it a little bit.

Write down the names of the people you *value* and *love* and the ones you *work* with the most (partner, family members, friends, team members...). Imagine that in 15 years, there's a party in your honour (and you are alive and kicking!). Each person is describing *why* they love and respect you. They may say just three words to summarize the interactions they had with you in life. What would you want those three words to be?

Next time you're with each of those people, approach your *time* with them as an opportunity to *demonstrate* those three qualities. Challenge yourself to *be* that person *now*.

Change-maker: just because

Do a generous act today for someone else, for the planet. Do not even think about getting a thank-you for it. Just do it because you want to give back. This could be as simple as sending a text message to someone in need, donating old (or new) clothes to someone, picking up some trash from the street, helping someone to cross the street.

4

ENERGY MANAGEMENT

How's your energy right here and now? Is it high or low? Do you know what gave you that energy or what took it away? In this chapter we will focus on managing our energy and on the art of moderation.

The Sanskrit word *brahmacharya* translates as 'the one who lives in constant awareness of the universe'. Literally, we translate *brahman* as 'pure consciousness, ultimate reality' and *charya* as 'the one who moves'. Walking with God, walking with pure energy, consciousness.

Celibacy?

Before we dive into energy management, we need to get something out of the way: very often, this principle is translated as 'celibacy', which would put off about 90% of Western Yoga practitioners. And, if it is true that there is a principle of celibacy in the Yoga philosophy, why is Yoga more popular than ever before? Why is nobody talking about this 'celibacy thing'?

Let there be no doubt, in the tradition of Patanjali and the audience he wrote it all for roughly 2,500 years ago, it definitely meant abstinence. Although little is known about his actual life, we do know that Patanjali was teaching to a predominantly male and ascetic audience.

Later on, however, significant teachers like Krishnamacharya proposed that the eight limbs of Yoga can be practised by everyone, by 'householders', women, all castes, anyone. In traditional India, a householder was typically an adult settled man with a family.

To fully understand this, we need to take a step back and look at Indian society in around 200 BCE. At that time, there were specific stages of life that were considered to be ideal. In the early part of life, up until the age of 25 or so, before marriage all time was devoted to study. Later on, one became a householder with a family life, of which sexual activity was part. Retreat was the next phase, followed by the life of a wandering ascetic.

If we compare this to the twenty-first century, we see that today's society is quite different. We can still find inspiration and guidance in this principle, though, as the main idea was to simply save energy to be able to study. Nowadays, we need all our attention to study or work, and to party, and to be a householder, and to go on retreats every now and then, and, and, and... but there's little attention on how we can save energy, let alone gather energy. In what follows, we zoom in on energy management in our modern age.

Energy, *prana, qi, chi, jing*, life force

Energy management will be one of the main ideas throughout this chapter, so what is *energy*? That's an easy question to answer, as everything is energy! Literally – everything. As everything is energy, perhaps that just made it all more complicated?

Energy has been and still is the subject of many sciences, but the answer you get depends on who you ask the energy question. In the context of this book, I don't want to go into mechanical energy, nuclear energy, solar energy and so on, for obvious reasons; however, I mention the different kinds of energy here as energy is so massively important in our daily lives. Solar energy might save the word, while nuclear energy has the potential to end the world we live in today.

In yogic terminology, energy is referred to as 'life force'. Without this energy, we could not live. It is not breath; it is not food or water; it is energy. If you run out of life force, what in Traditional Chinese Medicine we refer to as *jing* – your primal energy – you fully check out.

The word *prana* is one you might be familiar with, the Sanskrit equivalent to *ki (qi)*, *chi* or 'life force'. It runs through our veins, it makes us live. *Prana* is as real as emotion, thought and desire. Paul Grilley, the founder of Yin Yoga, told me during teacher training that 'the primary purpose of Yoga *asana* is to harmonize the flow of *chi* in your body'. As with breathing exercises, referred to as *pranayama* (control of the breath), what we want to accomplish is to balance the circulation of energy in the body. This will release stress, which is knots within the body, and will create space for self-inquiry to happen. We all know the 'sigh of relief' after finishing something. It's a natural thing to do and it unites body and mind.

Sexual energy

We started this chapter with an explanation that this principle does not equal celibacy, and we stay in the same atmosphere a little bit here as one of the biggest drainers of our energy is the sex impulse. It's very hard to find peace of mind when the mind is completely distracted by desires and attachments.

Most of us have sexual energy running through us. Becoming aware of it is quite crucial. When we feel sexual desire, we usually cling to it immediately. There's an instant attachment to it – it's so pleasurable that we want to hang on to it and never let it go. We want things to never change and we want to repeat everything that feels good about it. And that ignorance is exactly what causes our suffering. When it arises, it brings up sensations, feelings and then the 'stories' start; our mind goes crazy with 'stories'.

What we can do to counter this clinging is to accept all these feelings but not act on them. To simply be very comfortable with all these uncomfortable feelings.

There is nothing wrong with sexual desire and it's very hard to push it away. If you repress it, it will come back to you – probably disguised as something else – but it will get back to you tenfold.

There are certain desires that we might not want, that we might not like. But we can't repress them. We are all little rebels. If we can't do something, if it's forbidden, most of us are instantly drawn to it.

The rebel within

Imagine trying not to think of a purple goat. Ever. And especially not now, while you read. Please *do not* think of a purple goat.

The chances are that several purple goats have crept up in your thoughts already...

In essence, this principle has little to do with whether one is sexually active, single or married in the modern world. Avoiding sexual contact does not automatically make someone enlightened; on the contrary. If your mind is consistently haunted by sexual fantasies and frustrations, you are far from being a wise person.

Experiencing human love and relationships brings us the most valuable lessons about divine love, and life. (You can stop thinking about the purple goat now.)

Misuse of sexual energy often means that there is a secret somewhere. It's not by accident that this is our Fourth Principle, after non-harming, non-lying and non-stealing. When we continuously misuse sexual energy, for example, by desiring someone who is in a relationship with someone else, the mind knows, the body knows, the soul knows and it takes more energy away from us than we can ever imagine.

Let's now focus a little bit more on our energy management and what it means *to live in constant awareness with the universe*, as the literal translation of this principle teaches us.

Good vibes, bad vibes

Let's start with the energy we bring with us and the impact that we have on our general energy. In every interaction with another human Being, we exchange energy. There's the energy that we bring, the energy the other person brings and the energy that surrounds us. Energy ripples and radiates.

I can vividly remember visiting my grandmother, and she could have 'good days' or 'bad days'. A bad day would be one with a lot of pain, no eating, low energy and an overall lack of enthusiasm about life. The older she got, the higher the risk of a bad day, so I always prepared for it before visiting her. I would make sure that I felt rested, calm and strong before visiting and would never go there straight after landing, or straight after hosting a retreat – even though that was what was expected of me. I just didn't, because I knew that if I did that, we would all have a bad day. I would be tired; grandma would be tired and in pain; the overall energy would be low; thoughts might go to the past and the people we had lost. Food would be take-away, as neither of us felt like making something decent to eat and I would find myself crying all the way home, thinking about losing her soon, losing my own mom, feeling absolutely horrible. I can describe it very well as this happened more than once.

Instead, when I felt energetic, strong and balanced, I could share that energy with her. I would have more than enough energy to make dinner and she would eat all the 'vegetarian nonsense' I made her (when you have the money to buy meat, why on earth would you eat broccoli pie?). We would laugh a lot; she would have a little nap while I went for a walk in the not-so-vibrant city of Roosendaal. All good, everybody happy.

'The more you have, the more you can give'; this is surely true for our own energy. Think about it the next time you're visiting someone who might be ill or is going through a bad time. What is the energy you are going to bring to the 'party'?

The road to self-destruction

When we're low on energy, usually our minds aren't exactly vibing and thriving either. When we are unaware and mindless about this, we can get into a kind of bizarre mind trap, encouraging us to do even more of what deprives us of energy.

Let's say that someone you really like says something that hurts you. He or she knows you well and that remark just sliced through like a laser beam. The result is that your mind is now triggered and starts to question what they said. You start making up stories and adding drama. It might go like this: *Is it true? Am I really lazy and selfish? They don't love me. Nobody does. Pfff... I feel bad so I need to have something to make me feel better.*

What happens at this moment is that you start having all kinds of feelings that are uncomfortable. The ego, always there to protect us, wants to give us a way out of the negative feelings. It wants to help us, to guide us away from pain, instead of allowing whatever is there to be there, so that we are able to see what's going on – to become aware of the areas in our mind and spirit that need attention... instead of all that, in comes something else...

Let's go for chocolate and watch a series all night. I can't get myself to go to sleep now, after all this! I need the distraction now. Maybe I'll add a glass of wine, or six. And you can substitute chocolate with cookies, ice cream, beer – whatever your craving might be.

The tiny little problem with this avoidance behaviour, as an attempt to escape reality, is that after you have indulged in beer, ice cream and so on, you will probably feel much worse – physically, first, as none of this adds any energy to the body, but also mentally. You will probably notice that the feelings you wanted to avoid the most come back even stronger. A little bit like the purple goat idea, try to suppress it and, *nope, there it is again!* And if you're unlucky, you have now also added a feeling of shame and sadness about the situation you find yourself in.

The result of all this 'magic' is that it can go even further and lead to addiction, as in the example of late-night binge watching; you could find yourself quite sleep-deprived the next morning. You don't want to show up for work but you do, because you don't want to get fired. You might make a mistake here or there, though, which leads to negative remarks from your boss, clients or colleagues. And so, you're off again: *Is it true? Am I really lazy and selfish? You see, they don't love me. Nobody does. I feel bad so I need to have something to make me feel better tonight. Let's go for chocolate and watch a series all night…*

The bad remarks were an absolutely brilliant excuse to repeat the chocolate-binge-watching exercise again and again. Even though you know that this is the exact opposite of what you need. But, something is blocking you in your mind.

How to break free: pause, relax, reflect, act

Why is it that we know very well what is good for us and yet we do the exact opposite? Most people know exactly what they should or shouldn't eat to feel well. There's more information and guidance available about being healthy than ever before. Most people have a pretty good idea of the horrifying consequences of drinking, smoking, drugs and not moving your body. But still, we keep on ignoring this knowledge.

Why? Because we don't want to be uncomfortable. We run from the truth; we run from ourselves because we don't really know who we are. The ten principles and the Yoga philosophy, however, encourage us to pause before we open that chocolate bar, to pause when we want to take that glass of wine. They invite us to simply breathe for a second, so we can be aware of uncomfortable feelings.

One of the main definitions of Patanjali's take on Yoga is 'stilling the fluctuations of the mind'. Your desire to go for the chocolate or the wine, to escape a negative feeling, is nothing but a fluctuation. A fluctuation that can pass again.

Once we understand the mechanism of our own minds, we can start working with the mind and even start directing our thoughts. But, before anything else, we need to pause, relax and reflect before we act mindlessly.

Raise the standard

Our behaviour also reveals the standard we hold ourselves to, the standard when it comes to the kind of person we want to be. Without being too dramatic, it can't hurt to every now and then imagine that you have come to the end of your life, you have run out of life force and you ask yourself: *how do I want to look back at my life?*

During my work as a volunteer in a hospice in Belgium, I never heard someone say that they would have liked to have wasted more time. The stories that people told me in the last days of their lives were always about the people they had met and loved, and about their experiences.

While chocolate-wine-binge-watch evenings might seem like a good experience, let's just agree to not have too many of those nights or days. Call a friend who can make you laugh, start writing, make yourself something nice to eat, go for a walk, go to a Yoga class – even if that is the absolute last thing you want to do, do it anyway for yourself, because you are worth it. L'Oreal put it brilliantly in their marketing slogan, but it's true. Why not do those things for yourself, just *because you are worth it*? Because you are awesome! You are reading this book, so you must be really awesome.

Habits

We can examine which habits serve us and which don't, and in which areas of our lives we might need to create new habits. It's in that very moment of not going for the chocolate or wine – like in one of the previous examples – right at that moment that we can install a new habit. A habit that serves us in becoming the best version of ourselves, in raising that standard for ourselves.

Instead of mindlessly going for the chocolate, you notice the negative feeling you want to avoid and you reflect on it while doing something else. Make yourself do ten press-ups first, for example. That sounds ridiculous? Try it; I bet your desire for chocolate will be a lot less after doing or trying to do ten press-ups (not five, no, no, it's ten!).

Why? Because you will become very aware of how fit or unfit you are. If you're fit, you will probably want to stay that way. If you're not, it might be a good idea to become slightly more fit.

Is it really chocolate that I want right now or am I just bored, alone, thirsty or hungry? Pause, relax, reflect and take action. Instead of just going for a mindless action.

If you repeat the press-up action three times, I can assure you that the next time you want chocolate, there will be a moment of reflection. And this is exactly what we are seeking. Awareness.

A healthy habit

Some people claim that there is no such thing as a healthy habit. A habit is by definition something that you do rather mindlessly; you don't have to think about it any more. It is the opposite of mindful living, where you are aware of everything you do.

The ten principles of the Yoga philosophy by Patanjali aren't in any way about denying yourself the things you love. If you believe now that you can never have chocolate again, you have missed the point, or I haven't explained well. Completely denying yourself all things pleasurable would be violent and not in line with the very first principle of non-violence, which is always there as an underlying basis for all other principles. What the principles can teach us is to become more aware of our choices and desires, to figure out what is enough.

Moderation

When will you have enough food, sex, sleep, action, items in your house, goals reached, money in the bank, houses, partners? Moderation is for some the key to a happy life, when desire and addiction are seen as one of the main keys to suffering. There's a slightly different angle here than when we talked about greed in our previous chapter.

It's about desiring a glass of wine because you love wine and then, instead of emptying the entire bottle, just enjoying one glass. It's about having pasta because you crave it but skipping dessert to balance it out just a little bit.

I've come to understand that for most people the food examples are the easiest to grasp, but moderation can manifest itself in all aspects of life. Many people attend a Yoga retreat as an ideal moment to check in with some of their habits, for example.

Coffee addiction is probably the most common one on retreats. Just check in with yourself to see what happens to your body and mind when you don't have your cup of coffee in the morning, or when you have a lot less coffee. After the first day(s) of headache, it can be very interesting to observe if there is an actual change in how you feel.

It's just a job

A lot of people on my retreats and in my coaching sessions are completely overworked. They are giving way too much time to their boss, clients, patients, kids etc. This is basically like saying: *Oh, my free time is not that important. I'll just spend two hours less with my kids. I have more than enough time with them anyway.*

Let me give you a wake-up call here: there is never enough time to spend with your kids. They grow up quicker than you can blink! If your son is 12, you have about six, maybe eight more summers with him before he might set off and start his own life. If you don't have kids, you'll never get 'time' back. You age every minute that you work. It's time with which you could have done something really cool, for yourself.

And, I'm really sorry to break it to you: your boss will fire you on the spot if she or he needs to. Without blinking. If you are your own boss, you can go bankrupt.

If you're in a medical profession, you could mess up, your medical board could mess up. Whatever situation you find yourself in, it can always change. Security and control within a job is an illusion.

It's just a job. Oh my God, I can remember the day that this very spiritual lady in a tent in the Wadi Rum desert of Jordan gave me that message. There she was, all dressed in white, Miss Super-Yogi, with her so-called non-physical guide telling me that the thing that defined me was *just a job.* Honestly? I wanted to slap her. At that moment, my job meant the world to me. It had given me confidence, a big car, a high salary, awesome experiences, cool colleagues, a cool boss, opportunities, friends, freedom; *you can hardly call that 'just a job'!*

She then asked me if the job paid my rent. She had to ask three times, as I didn't (want to) understand the question. Finally, I mumbled out that *yes, of course, it paid the rent.* 'Well then, isn't that just a job?' And now, all these years later, behold the irony; I am so grateful for those words and I repeat them often – usually when I'm dressed in white after handing out angel cards and probably annoying the heck out of some people with my spiritual *bla-bla.* Big smile!

If your job currently defines you, re-read the previous paragraph. Whatever job you do, whatever the responsibilities, money, power, importance, it truly is *just a job,* which means that there are other, more important things. A job just pays the rent or the mortgage. Family, friends, love, contribution and service to others mean so much more.

Are you overworked?

Resentment, tightness, anger, restlessness and frustration might be an indication. These feelings are not about who we are, nor about the frequency we want to be at. You may also notice how your breathing is shallow. When these conditions are present, you might need to calm down. Take a couple of deep breaths, step back and observe what you are trying to do. Find balance in your work life. Work–life balance. This is old-school terminology, but so needed.

Focus

I have no idea who came up with this quote, so I'm not deliberately stealing by not acknowledging. I really don't know, but Tony Robbins brought it to my attention years ago: 'Where attention goes, energy flows.'

During your meditation or Yoga practice, it's very interesting to focus on your energy. On the kind of energy that you bring into the practice. Is it an energy of compassion and love for yourself? Is it nice and calming, or is it something else?

Whenever you are pushing yourself – or spacing out, for that matter – be conscious about these energies and bring your attention back to the mat, back to your practice. Bring your full attention to what you feel and *where* you feel *what*. With every single distraction, bring that attention back.

By giving attention to a distraction, you are giving it the liberty to be there. The same goes for negative thoughts. It's only natural that something negative pops up every now and then, but there is a time and place for these thoughts. When you are not zooming in on them on your mat, when they are not invited to be there, you make room for energy to flow to other places.

What do you wish to give attention to, energy to? What do you choose to focus on? *I don't want this to happen. I'm afraid that it will happen.* What exactly? Keep mentioning it, keep giving it attention and you're well on your way towards it.

Once upon a time, I had a beautiful motorbike: a BMW 1200 GS. I told you before, I was a proper snob; it was all about the big brands and appearances in my past corporate life. (Although, I still find this to be the coolest bike in the universe. I don't even own a camel now – nothing – but this is totally beside the point.) The number-one lesson in learning to drive is what to focus on when things don't go as planned. Don't look at the tree if you don't want to smash into the tree. This is exactly the same in living a conscious life: focus your attention on where you want to go.

What are you focusing on? What will you do when you succeed in whatever it is? Do you have a vision of that? Is that really what you want, or is that something that the outside world made you think you want? Do you focus on the hurdles, and the *what-ifs*?

Who wants to live forever?

Energy management gives us a specific result, according to the *Yoga Sutras*. The result of having healthy energy management is gaining great energy and power and maybe even living longer. Some commentaries even go further and interpret this as being able to choose when you die – something that, after my work at the hospice, I strongly believe in. I have seen it happen: people who 'wait' for a certain far-away family member to pop in just before they depart. These are not stories, but real-life experiences that I can vouch for.

Connection fail: we are all energy

As we know, one of the definitions of Yoga is 'union', which is ultimately what we all strive for – more connection with ourselves, more union with the people we love, with the people we work with, and maybe even with strangers. Strong connection-based relationships will give you immense highs and the deepest lows, which is all energy. It's like an emotional rollercoaster without a beginning or an end, and it can be more intense than anything else. I feel so incredibly fortunate to have experienced this rollercoaster a couple of times, while at the same time nothing has caused me more pain.

What follow are some very vulnerable lines. I'm writing them down for you as perhaps you can relate to some of the feelings. Yes, you might argue that this is a hidden form of therapy, to share these thoughts with the world, and yes, I fully agree; it's not even hidden that well.

It hurts. Every single day that I can't connect with you, it hurts.

Am I being punished?

What is it that I need to learn?

What do we need to learn?

Is there even a 'we'?

Do I hang on and see where this all goes, or do I need to let go?

Do I show unconditional love, drop all expectations and just be with it?

Or, do I need to set my boundaries, reasoning that I have the right to know what you feel and that you just need to learn how to express your feelings?

Can we ever make this work?

Is it even love when we need to make it work?

Is love work?

You are so different to me; why did you ever show up in my life?

Oh, right, I invited you in, very literally.

I regret that day so much.

I'm so grateful for that day.

Thank you.

We (*me*, in the story above) tend to ignore the fact that we are already one with other people, so we can never be separated. There's an energetic unity that connects us all. In that sense, you can never let go of someone, without letting go of yourself.

What you can do, however, is let go of the drama. Letting go of the storylines we so desperately want to create and cling to. The more we want to believe our stories, the further we will be from our true Self.

The only thing you can do to avoid the control trap is to step back. To once again pause, relax, reflect and take action, or not. To fully accept the situation and the other person as a person, or not. This part is as much about non-attachment as it is about energy management, which makes it a brilliant transition towards our next chapter on *aparigraha,* or 'non-attachment'.

Change-maker: what gives you energy?

Take a moment right now and jot down five things that turbo-charge you with energy. Write down five more things that cosmically charge you. Make a little list of five things that energize you. Smile while you note down five things that make you happy when doing them.

Do at least one thing out of your list of 20, *today*, and *plan* to do at least five other things really soon.

When we feel fatigued, sometimes all it takes is to realize that we are not doing the things that usually energize us.

5

NON-ATTACHMENT

It is what it is; just let go. This little phrase is the ultimate way to spiritually bypass just about any situation we encounter. I hear coaches and people who mean well saying it all the time, but I believe it can do more damage than good when misused. If you don't focus on why people feel shaken up in certain situations in the first place, you're missing a massive clue in finding more peace of mind.

Our next principle is all about the concept of letting go, and our inspiration comes from the yogic principle of *aparigraha*, which translates as 'non-grasping', 'non-possessiveness', 'non-clinging', 'non-greed' or 'non-attachment'. Patanjali advises us to practise 'greedlessness' in three different verses of the *Yoga Sutras*, so this fifth principle definitely demands more in-depth understanding.

The Second Noble Truth (of Buddhism) teaches us that attachment or clinging is the main cause of all of our human suffering; therefore, the topic of non-attachment can't be anything else but exciting to explore.

We can be attached to so many things in our daily lives. We can be attached to people, things, our own body, ideas, experiences, situations and so on. Let's dive in!

People

Have you ever noticed that we really claim some people to be our possessions in most languages? We refer to *my* kids, *my* partner, *my* boss, *my* patients, *my* friends, *my* students, *my* teachers and so on. Technically speaking, however, we have no ownership over our partner, boss, patients, friends, students or teachers, not even over our kids. Taking it further, we could say that nothing is here for us and we don't have the right to own anything on this planet.

Relationships

We believe that our happiness lies in the relationship itself, with the idea in mind that *if I never let go, the relationship will never change.* This is not true, because it ignores the impermanence of relationships. Everything constantly changes – our world, our bodies and thus our relationships.

Things

Morocco is very traditional in many aspects, and one tradition that I have really started to appreciate is to have an empty kitchen. There's hardly any hoarding when it comes to packaged food, cans or any other plastic rubbish. As lots of women are still at home all day, they have time to go to the markets and make almost everything themselves.

There's no need for a big fridge or a freezer, because you give away what you don't use yourself. Left-over food goes to other people in the streets, and afterwards cats and dogs can have a go at it. The killer seagulls come last, just before it gets picked up by the garbage truck. You don't shop for an entire week and then throw half of it away when the date is overdue because you didn't eat it all. You only buy what you need, and only when you run out of food do you buy again.

Three-day menus

We all have very busy lives and, most likely, you don't live in Morocco. But, why not make a menu for two days of the week? Or three days? It's very simple; you will eat more consciously and buy less. You buy what you need and when it's all gone – and only then – do you go out and buy more. That is conscious living, conscious buying and being aware of what you buy and consume.

The dress

Losing your suitcase on a holiday is one of the best things that can happen. Sure, the first days, it's quite inconvenient that you can't wear that special sweater you bought for the trip, and you don't have your own shampoo or conditioner. If you travel to a warm country still wearing your winter jeans and boots, of course you're not thrilled – but it can also be so liberating.

I will never forget hosting one of the Costa Rica retreats, where we had one woman wearing the same dress for all activities, for about five days. The airline lost her suitcase and so she bought this cool red dress. I thought it was a bit odd in the beginning as I wouldn't have bought a dress for a Yoga retreat but, quite frankly, we should have framed it right there and then after the retreat. What an incredible investment! It served as a bathing suit, evening gown, Yoga outfit, beach dress, pyjamas; it was washed over and over as it easily dried in those jungle temperatures. It was brilliant and she started to feel more and more comfortable every day, with just the dress.

Non-possessiveness can be a tricky topic, as it doesn't mean that we can't have any possessions. It's when we get completely attached to our possessions that we end up in trouble. It's when we buy because we feel a void, when we try to get rid of uncomfortable feelings and distract ourselves by buying more stuff, that we suffer. The Yoga philosophy can teach us to step away from quick satisfaction and briefly check with ourselves when we are about to buy something. *Why do I want to buy this right now? Or get four of them in different colours? Is it good for me? Is it good for the environment? Was it made in a fair way or was there violence involved* (our first principle)*? Did somebody or something suffer for me to be able to buy this?*

It's about simply becoming a little bit more aware of our buying behaviour instead of mindlessly going through the motions and hoarding more stuff. Throughout this book you will read this and many other variations on becoming more aware. I'm very aware that I'm repeating certain things over and over again. It's because I'm so convinced about their importance and the impact that these ideas can have on your day-to-day life. If you want more peace of mind in your life, you need to learn how to pause, relax and reflect instead of mindlessly reacting to your every feeling or emotion.

Unfortunately, as with many things, even the non-attachment principle has been commercialized in a way. Nowadays, a lot of people are aware of all kinds of techniques on how to de-clutter their homes – but let's not get so busy with our wardrobe cleaning that we forget to de-clutter our mind. It's still pretty interesting to check feelings like shame, guilt, emptiness and so on that might have triggered us to buy stuff in the first place. More on this later, but whenever we have those kinds of impulses, we should welcome them and investigate them! It's the only way to reach more peace of mind.

I believe, so I am

This is who I am. I hear people say it all the time. *I am just stubborn, always have been and always will be.* I disagree. Being stubborn is demonstrating a behaviour, and you have simply repeated this behaviour enough times during your life to believe that stubbornness is one of the characteristics that defines you. It gives you the perfect excuse to not change anything about that behaviour. Just know that if you want to change this behaviour because it doesn't serve you any more, you can.

'You have to work hard for the money.' 'Money doesn't come easy.' 'All men are...' 'All women are...' 'I didn't go to college, so I am not smart.'

All of the sentences above are beliefs. And we tend to cling to them very tightly. The same goes for our ideas, views and opinions. Are you open enough to have other people's ideas change you? Do you dare listen?

> If you realize that all things change, there is nothing you will try to hold on to.
>
> *Lao Tzu*

I know several people who are always in between holidays. This can be fun, of course, when it is to travel the world and explore, but it is also interesting if it's about filling a void or ignoring a lack of peace of mind in their own homes, or in their own environment. They try to keep the holiday memory alive for as long as they can and as soon as the memory starts to fade, they renew the experience by booking another holiday. By going away and escaping, they are constantly looking forward to the next thing. Trying to hold on to the feeling that travelling gives. This will make it hard for them to be *in the now*, and not to get attached to experiences.

Meet Marwan

As you know by now, my job once defined me. I was proud of my hotshot function title and I started to *slightly* (OK, a lot) look down on people who were less 'fortunate' than me. Today, I find role models all over and I couldn't care less about titles.

There's a particular waiter in one of the Moroccan venues that I rent in Marrakesh who I would like to introduce to you here: meet Marwan. Marwan is usually smiling and he seems to be genuinely happy. You can even notice by the laughter around when his shift has started. On several occasions, I have seen some guests (none of our yogis, of course) treat him very disrespectfully – or, what I would label as disrespectful. Basically, they instructed him to do things without any form of 'please' or 'thank you' and it was all rather directive and in a loud voice, as if he had a hearing problem. This is me wording it in the most non-violent way I can; just imagine them barking instructions.

'If someone lashes out at you, they have a problem, not you.' I doubt if he has ever heard these words of Abraham and Esther Hicks, but he damn well practises them to perfection. The negative actions of the guests don't seem to upset him at all. By the time he turns around and walks away from the *lovely bunch*, his face is all smiley again.

It's obvious that he is very happy doing this job at the moment, but I also believe that if he needed to, he would change jobs and continue to be happy. He is clearly not defined by his job and, above all, his happiness doesn't depend on others. There's an intrinsic happiness from within and it shows. It radiates.

Self-image

We age. *Hallelujah!* That is a really good thing. Of course, the utter grief comes one day when you look into that mirror and start realizing that you are ageing and losing what you have defined up until then as your beauty. And no matter what all the spiritual books may say about it, it's not a happy moment. Yes, probably most of us are very grateful to have made it to a certain age and at the same time we face a massive *but*, as at first there is little bliss in wrinkles, grey hairs, upset hormones, physical changes, 'general decay' and the overall transition to a new phase in your life. Allow all of the emotions that come with this transition to be the first step towards accepting it. As anything, this phase will also pass.

Anicca (the 'cc' is pronounced 'ch', as in church) in Pali encompasses impermanence, and this term is often used in meditation courses. After sitting for a while in a meditation pose, you start to feel all kinds of physical discomfort. A shoulder playing up, sleeping feet, tingling somewhere or everywhere; there could be many different things screaming very loudly for your attention. When you can reach back to the knowledge that everything passes, you might feel relief. Why not give it a go and try to use it, on and off the mat?

Anicca, anicca, anicca, also this will pass. Impermanence is part of life but we do not accept it. We know very well that everything is constantly evolving; we have just aged while simply reading these pages... The time that passed in the last five minutes is never coming back. Impermanence is inevitable. It's meeting and departing, it's life and death and falling in and out of love.

And still. We will not accept it and have 'I love you forever' tattooed on our bodies. Knowing that there is no *forever*. It's just that this moment is so great that we want to hold on tight. Things should never change, so we hold on tighter. If we could just stop the struggle and allow change to happen, we could replace the struggle with simple, pure joy.

Connection fail: caring

So why do we cling to certain people, things, beliefs and situations? Alan Wallace says the following.

> *What fundamentally drives us is caring. We care about what we identify with. Our skin, family, country, community... When and if your happiness is based on your attachments and clinging, grabbing on to them, you're in for tragedy. We have no control over wealth, fame, power, beauty, etc. We think we do but we don't.*

The problem is that wealth, fame, power and beauty are often seen as indicators of success in modern societies, which leaves a lot of people being tortured by their own minds as intense desires are projected in a faraway future. When you add the feeling that most of it will never happen, it's easy to become frustrated and depressed because others seem to manage to have what you want.

It's important to know that a sense of general wellbeing is not dependent on whether or not pleasant things are happening to us or not. Being mentally balanced means that we can be happy with and without all the *hedonic pleasures*.

How to manifest your desires

When people are new to my coaching, they very often come in feeling confused as these days there is a lot of attention being given to how to manifest your dreams and desires. But, doesn't Buddhism tell us that all of our suffering is caused by our desires? So, how to manifest them? Or, should we not desire anything, ever?

Let's go back for a moment and start with a definition. Merriam Webster's definition of a 'desire' tells us that it is 'a conscious impulse towards something that promises enjoyment or satisfaction in its attainment'. From this definition we could already learn that the desire in itself is not the reason for our suffering. To have desires is not bad. The desire to have more peace of mind, for example, to have blissful moments, is a desire in itself but it's not necessarily bad for us.

Desires make us passionate about reaching our goals, desires push us forward and there's absolutely nothing wrong with that. It is the attachment to the fulfilment of the desire that brings us suffering. If your stream of thoughts is all about feeling good once you have this or that, this means that you see the desire far away in the future. This also means that you are clinging and grasping on to the desire as the *fulfilment* of the desire, and that only this will make you happy.

In my coaching sessions, we really take the time to focus on every single step; here I will share the steps you should follow to manifest your every desire.

1. Know what you want and why you want it.

2. Know where it all starts.

3. Know exactly where you want to go. What you want in your life. Most people start by telling me what they *don't* want – instantly. I don't want to be poor any more. I don't want to be overweight. I don't want to be like my father. And while this is good to know, it doesn't tell me what you do want and why. Typically, a therapist will not ask you directly why, but you can easily ask yourself why you want something. After the first answer that comes to your mind, ask again: why? And again: why? I want more money. What does

'more' mean? 1 million US dollars. Why? To feel safe. Why do you want to feel safe? I hate being in debt. Why? It makes me feel like a loser. Why? In a session, I would probably first focus on the numbers. How did you get to the 1 million figure? Is it based on actual calculations or are you just shouting out something (as you don't think it's doable anyway)?

4. Know and feel that your desire will manifest itself. In this phase you check your limiting beliefs. What is blocking you? How are you sabotaging yourself? Are you letting in the right vibration? I want to make more money but I don't want to become like those rich people who only care about themselves. I don't believe you can become wealthy and not lie and cheat. I am ready for a relationship but, I don't want him or her to be short, tall, fat, skinny, ugly, old, young, divorced, with odd hobbies.

I am not letting myself get hurt again – no way. I want to become healthy but, I don't want to exaggerate and become a health freak. I want to lose weight but not too much in my face or I will look so much older, get wrinkles etc. I want it... but I don't want it... This is exactly the same as saying 'no' to the universe. It's like saying 'yes' and 'no' at the same time.

Creating smoke

Saying 'yes' and 'no' at the same time is like pressing the gas and brake pedals at the same time, and that is very bad for a car engine. Your rear wheels might spin and you create a lot of smoke but you move neither forwards nor backwards (newer cars will not even allow you to do this).

Your physical engine is your heart. Accelerating and braking – saying 'yes' and 'no' at the same time – costs energy. It's really bad for the heart and, most importantly, absolutely nothing happens besides creating a lot of drama (smoke)!

5. Build up a regular concentration/meditation practice. Simply concentrating on your breathing for a couple of minutes a day will give you the extra space that you need to find more peace of mind. Try to quieten the mind, to avoid bringing in more limiting beliefs and to notice when you are behaving in a way that is not aligned with what you really want. Concentration and meditation will make you more aware of your daily actions and thoughts.

6. Visualize. If you can't visualize what it looks like when your desires have manifested themselves,

how can it ever become real? Most of the top athletes will have some kind of a visualization practice to tap into their inner strength and make body and mind conscious of the possibility of reaching a goal.

7. Feel. Truly connect with the feeling of having accomplished your desire. A step further than mentally visualizing accomplishment is truly tapping into the feeling of manifesting your desire.

8. Do the work. It's remarkable how many people forget this step! If you want to have a fitter body, you have to put in the effort to actually exercise the body. If you want to become a famous writer, you have to actually write. If you want to sell something, you will have to actually get out there and do some promoting of your product or service. 'Sit back, relax and enjoy the ride' is not applicable in this phase.

9. Trust. Personally, I think this is the most important step of them all. You need to trust in yourself and in life that things will work out in the end. You might not know why it feels like you're side-tracking at times, but trust that you're on your way and keep going. You do the work and keep trusting, which means that you're also fine when your desires do not come through, because you're enjoying and

embracing the entire road trip. If what you envisioned happens, great. If it doesn't, also great. If this last sentence still leaves you a little puzzled, keep reading; it will become clearer in what follows.

My 40th birthday: a manifesting case study

To celebrate my 40th birthday I had visualized a villa in Ibiza, the island I loved from hosting so many Yoga retreats there. If you're not familiar with it, Ibiza is a very special little island. It's part of Spain but nothing like Spain; Ibiza is Ibiza.

I envisioned a private and brilliant chef, who would know me well and make all my favourite dishes; for me, this is the ultimate way to feel wealthy. There would be a cool Jeep involved (I still appreciate cars – going yogi didn't change that) and friends would come and visit. Mom would be there and everyone would just need to pay for the flight; I would take care of all the rest.

I wanted this partially because, for some reason, I had never been to one of those foreign-country weddings or parties, and also because I really wanted to celebrate my 40th birthday. Not everyone makes it to that age. Instead of bitching about the rather visible ageing effects (*yes – serious vanity alert*) I decided to celebrate 40 years of being on planet earth.

I visualized this idea for about two years; I felt how it would feel walking around the villa, how I would feel driving to the airport to pick up a friend from the US (no idea who exactly, just an idea). And here's the fun part: I envisioned it when reality was telling me that there was no way that this would ever come true. Looking at my business figures, it would be one round of champagne at a local café in Antwerp as business was quite OK; but I literally made all – yes all – the rookie mistakes in the book on how to start your own business. And still, how magically everything started to shift in the following two years!

I just knew it was going to happen; I felt it, and I left *the how* to the universe.

Some call it a universal manager: you brief him or her and trust they will do the job. The crux is in the trust. Do you really trust? Or, will you start interfering? Preventing little disasters from happening? It's no different than a director giving instructions to a manager. You have to be very clear, and after that you need to trust.

Why this long story? Not to brag – God no, there are thousands of people who can do this, easily, with a bigger villa and much more bling. I'm sharing my story as I am no different to you. If I can do this, so can you.

The empty-seats guru

Maybe you don't want to rent a villa in Ibiza; you want something completely different. Whatever it is, you need to start experimenting, as that's what I did in my years, working up towards the whole Ibiza experience.

I have been sharing this experiment for years on my retreats, and I can't even count the number of ecstatic emails I have received ever since I brought up this topic. It's about my famous trip to Costa Rica and flying business class, without paying for it. This is how it started.

Just before the Costa Rica retreat started, we were having a coffee somewhere in town and in the corner there was one book that really grabbed my attention: *Ask and It Is Given* by Esther and Jerry Hicks. I had vaguely heard about Abraham, but this book had an attraction like no other and I started reading – and kept reading. I was fascinated and at the same time slightly sceptical towards this version of the Law of Attraction theory.

Whenever I have doubts about something, I usually try it for a while and then make my mind up about it. The same goes with this theory, so I started imagining flying back in business class. We had the cheapest tickets with an airline I had never flown with before, so a free upgrade was unrealistic. Business class was something I appreciate for long hauls, though, and I had good memories from my corporate days when I would pay for it myself on my holidays to ridiculously far-off destinations. 'Saving' was a dirty word in those days, and I enjoyed spending every cent I earned.

The fun of this experiment was that I was really following all the steps (similar to the ones I described above) and at the same time I learned to also let it go. If the business class were to happen, I would be thrilled; if it didn't, that would also be fine. It's just a seat (and champagne. I love champagne, but never mind).

Of course, during our three-week stay, I didn't receive a spontaneous email from the airline to inform me that I was miraculously upgraded to business class. But, I was still convinced that good things were going to happen. On our departure day, we came to the check-in and noticed a lot of buzz, and some drama left and right. The drama was that most flights were overbooked – hence the question: would we like to fly business class on one of the next flights? *Hooray! It had worked!* Long story short, we didn't accept it; it was unclear when we would arrive in Brussels with several connecting flights, but it had worked. This experiment completely kicked off my journey with the Law of Attraction.

You don't believe me? Give it a try on your next flight; imagine at least one empty seat next to you so you have more space. Follow the steps I gave you earlier. Once you have achieved this, next time go for an upgrade and imagine that. Make sure you get back to me; I absolutely love hearing about these stories!

I can only invite you to dive into the book *Ask and It Is Given*, especially if you're rather sceptical. In what follows, I will highlight two often-heard critiques.

That's not what I meant!

We tend to get exactly what we want. The problem is that we didn't make our *order* clear enough to the universe. I remember very clearly one of my worst examples of this one.

I put it out there one day to the universe to fall in love – as in seriously fall in love, that feeling, that rush. It can be such an experience. I really wanted to feel that way again. And I did. I met a very interesting person with an even more interesting love life. What I forgot to mention to the big mighty universe is that it would be nice if this person was honest, had values, was not married and would not play me for a complete fool (*Oh, didn't I say I was married?*).

But I hadn't asked for that, had I? In retrospect, I know that I had asked for the wrong thing altogether. But, I learned my lesson well. I also realized that *what comes to you always matches you* (again, thank you Esther Hicks and Abraham for these words of wisdom). I had created this; I had pursued this person's attention and honesty wasn't exactly my own go-to value in those days either.

This stuff doesn't work!

In *Ask and It Is Given*, Esther and Jerry Hicks give a vivid picture of why this stuff *does* work. They talk about how simple it is in essence to travel from Phoenix, Arizona to San Diego, California: 'if you will face in the direction of San Diego, and continue to move in the direction of San Diego, then you must reach San Diego'. But what, they say, if you keep getting confused and heading back towards Phoenix? Will you ever actually get there? It's a ridiculous question, they say. 'Because of your knowledge of direction, and with the help of road signs and other travelers, it is not logical that you would remain forever lost in the Arizona desert unable to find your way to San Diego. The 400-mile trip between the two cities is easily understood, and the idea of making the trip is completely believable, and if it were your desire to make the trip, you would find a way to do so.' It is just as easy, they say, to make the trip between where you are now and where you want to be, once you learn to read the signs along the way, and understand why you may have turned back or gone in the wrong direction.

I love this road example as it makes total sense. If we continue on the right road, we will arrive; we must arrive. What we don't realize in our daily lives is when we turn around regarding the things that we desire.

At what point do you keep turning around when it comes to financial wellbeing? At what point do you turn around in your relationships? People can't get too close because of *what* exactly? Feelings of loneliness or knowing that you *should* open up a bit more creep up – so, you turn around... back to Phoenix.

This 'turning around' is causing you to waste so much *petrol*. Your engine is running on overtime, and remember: your heart is your engine. You feel drained, you blame work, stress, your parents, your childhood, your dog and next door's parrot. But it might not be these things that are really the cause of fatigue.

Once you understand and get clarity on how you are sabotaging yourself in *getting to San Diego*, you will not do it again. To be able to understand, we need clarity; we must first find a little bit more peace of mind, to embrace ourselves and all our flaws.

When we concentrate and meditate, we make time to do exactly that, so we can become aware of our thoughts – of the thoughts that serve us (to San Diego) or not (back to Phoenix).

Why, oh why?

Why do we get attached? Why do we keep thinking that fulfilling our every desire would make us happy? One could write six books about that, but one thing that *messes us all up* is our modern definition of being successful.

For most people, the concept of success is nowadays defined by the amount of things we have. We all seem to need loads of stuff, the perfect job, the perfect relationship, the perfect friends and the perfect hobbies in order to be successful and thus *happy*. Basically, there's an understanding that our happiness depends on what we possess.

And do you know what I find the most interesting about all this? That most people fully realize that the above is not true! They know very well that more stuff will not make them any happier, yet still so many keep up the pursuit of *more*. Could it be because there is no alternative definition that appeals?

I often get the remark that *I have it easy* because I live in a warm country, choose how I live my life and work whenever I want. *It's easy for me* because I don't have a mortgage (I do, by the way) or a partner (I have that too) or kids (nope, not those) – and we can't all move to Morocco, can we?

Well, Morocco has loads of space so you're most welcome, but that was *my* choice and it might not be your idea of a nice country to live in. The thing is that by simply comparing our lives to other people's lives, we continue not grounding ourselves nor feeling which choices will make us happier. So, is there a way out of the madness of possessions? Yes, gratitude is our antidote.

Count your blessings

When you start focusing on what you have instead of what is lacking, your perspective, if you allow it, can change instantly. It's extremely difficult to feel frustrated when you feel truly grateful. Very simply:

when you have a feeling of abundance, you will feel a lot better than when you focus on a lack of something.

It will be hard to find a self-development book that doesn't mention gratitude, so there must be some truth in the act of counting your blessings being an antidote for feeling bad. Why not give it a try? Just check, right here and now: what are you grateful for? And if life is testing you right now and life is a bit *sh***? Just be grateful that you can read this book, which I wrote for you. And smile. For the sake of it, why not experiment with this for a couple of days? In the morning, why not be grateful for one or two simple things? Just try it out. Will you have instant, life-changing, mind-blowing results? Maybe, just maybe.

Generosity, just because

What was the last thing you gave away?

Perhaps you gave something to or did something for someone, but after a while you were upset because they didn't express their gratitude. In that case, your giving wasn't pure generosity. You expected something back.

And yes, you can bring in the element of fundamental politeness. Or, *they could have said something*. Yes and no and maybe. If you give from the heart because you want to give, you don't expect anything back. Not even a word. This is pure non-attachment.

If you are really generous, you don't need people to thank you. Your ego doesn't need to hear the words because it was about the giving, not the reaction it could have provoked.

Our third principle of non-stealing and this principle of non-attachment are linked in that they both make us aware of our generosity. When you are generous and truly give from the heart, this is when you are a truly *rich* person.

Why we are here

In the *Yoga Sutra* on non-attachment, we read that the result of non-grasping is to discover why we were born. By letting go of the body and all thoughts, we create space and are like the Buddha in his awakening; the story goes that he could see all his past lives because he created this space to exist. Patanjali had the same idea; we can see our past lives because we have moved on. We are an embodied Being but we are not solely attached to the body as such. It's just a vehicle to transport us on our path.

Perhaps theories about past lives may be a bit farfetched for you, but having a clear view or sense of trust about the path, our reason for being 'here', could alleviate a whole lot of pain and worry for a lot of people. It's then that we realize that it's OK to be less attached to life itself.

Allow life to happen

One of the things that I learnt during my time volunteering at a palliative ward is that there really is but one certainty in life, and that is that we will die. This idea developed an unexpected depth when I saw people dying on a regular basis.

It was my own fear and fascination with death that had brought me to volunteer at this place. Sometimes people were still struggling and fighting when there were all the physical signs that their time was up. Other times, I saw people departing in the most peaceful way I could imagine. It's about allowing life and death to happen. Maybe we can't always entirely choose how we die, but we can for sure choose how we live.

If we stop resisting and just allow life to happen, we are stepping away from control and we are permitting life to be just as it is. When we can let go of the attachment to the idea of how life should be, we can start enjoying life a little bit more.

Allowing life to be 'as is' doesn't mean that we can't feel or long for something, or be passionate; on the contrary, it can make us even more passionate about life!

Indifference

Non-attachment is not the same as becoming disassociated with the world around you. It is not the same as indifference; as a matter of fact, it's exactly the opposite. It's actually becoming more connected with our world, but with more engagement. If Yoga means union, our non-attachment can create more union with the world around us as we can see everything from a more generous perspective.

So far, we have discussed five principles, often bundled as *yama*: non-violence, truthfulness, non-stealing, energy management and non-attachment. Actively cultivating these principles brings us closer to our true nature. When we have a pure and balanced mind, we don't want to harm ourselves or other people; we don't lie; we don't steal; we know when it's enough and we are generous with what we have. Once again, these principles are not instructions on what we can't do – they are but an encouragement to actively live a meaningful life.

In the next five chapters, we will focus on the five *niyama* of the Yoga philosophy, starting off with our sixth principle: purity.

Change-maker: three very simple questions to ask yourself

What are you holding on to that you no longer need? What possesses you? How can you simplify your life?

Change-maker: same-same but different

To practise non-attachment, you will need to step out of your comfort zone at times. If there's rigidness to a practice or a teacher, that might stand in the way of your growth. Why not experiment and take a different class? Try a different teacher? If you have certain routines in your life, tweak them, just to learn to experiment and to grow. If you're not attached, you can easily change and observe if your habits and fixed routines still serve you. If they serve you, great – bring them back. If they don't, change what you need to change.

6

PURITY

With the next principle, we move on to *niyama*. While the previous five principles have been more about our interaction with the world, the next five centre on the relationship that we have with ourselves. In the context of this book, however, we will look at all the principles from both perspectives.

The principle of purity is derived from the Sanskrit word *saucha*, which means 'cleanliness' or 'purity'. In this chapter, we will learn about cleanliness of the body, our environments and our psychological hygiene, which will lead us to the topic of meditation.

Through purification, we attain a state of more harmony and balance so that we become aware of who we really are. In essence, we are all pure. With this principle, we learn how to get rid of whatever can potentially pollute our body and mind, so we are able to see a glimpse of our true Self, with a capital 'S'. Turn it around and it's easy to understand that with impurity, toxicity or a disturbed body and mind, we simply cannot discover nor realize the best version of our Self.

Stinky business

Let's start with the most obvious: cleanliness of the body. During my very first teacher training in India many years ago, we had to try all kinds of different cleansing techniques. Maybe you are familiar with *jala neti* (literally 'nose cleanse'), where you put warm and slightly salted water into one nostril and it comes out the other to cleanse the nose? Or *sutra neti* ('thread'), where you replace the water with a thread, stick it into your nose, grab it at the back of your throat and floss? A not-so-joyful experience, but I swear that I saw and heard better afterwards. Because of my history of ten years of heavy migraines and vomiting, I'm not a fan of the one where you drink salty water to vomit your guts out. In my opinion – and I'm not a doctor – the digestive system is made in a way that things go down, not up. If food does come up, it's because the body wants to get rid of it on its own, and there's no reason for us to force it.

There are many different techniques to clean your nose, mouth, eyes, bowels and so on. Breathing techniques (*pranayama*) and Yoga postures (*asanas*) are also seen as purifying techniques. *Panchakarma* (the cleansing my mom underwent in Sri Lanka) is a three-week programme, the main idea of which is purification.

As the body is a collection of chemicals, purifying it sounds like a good idea, but my inner nerd instantly wants to jump in, of course, and question why we would need purification. Detoxing is a very fashionable thing to do these days, but does that mean that our body and mind are dirty? And, if we stick to very clean input, do we still need to purify? These are interesting questions.

It's not just what goes into our body that is important; what comes out is just as important. And while there's tremendous wisdom about our bodies' condition in fresh faeces and urine, that is not what I mean. If we move away from the physical aspect of purity and zoom in more on our psychological and mental hygiene, things can become really interesting.

Just quickly check in here with the words that you speak, for example. That kind of output, the language that you use – is it quite clean, or not so much? How do you speak to and about other people? What do you usually talk about? Is there a lot of chitchat and just filling the air around you with words, or do you only speak when you have something interesting to say?

This has everything to do with the principle of purity – paying attention to our behaviour, to the words we speak. This is a way to purify ourselves and to discover who we really are.

The power of silence

Throughout this book, you'll notice that I'm an advocate of silent retreats for various reasons, and using silence to purify our speech is one of them. When we leave out verbal communication with other people, it's quite refreshing to notice what we would like to say if we could or would talk.

On a silent retreat, we frame the situation of solitude: to be on our own, with our own thoughts, and to take away as much distraction as possible.

Chatterbox

Are you a chatterbox who doesn't really say much?

Some people talk a lot but don't share a thing, and some people ask a million questions but never really answer any. Of course, one could say this is because they are so empathic and want to know all about the other person, but is this really true? Could the talking or questioning be a façade to avoid showing who they really are?

Digital detox

On most silent retreats, there is some kind of policy around the use of mobile phones and interaction with the outside world. It used to be all fancy to be busy and connected, but now it's a full-on luxury to go offline, voluntarily, for more than a day – let alone for ten full days, or even longer.

On the silent retreats that I host, I ask people to hand over their phones. This condition is mentioned on the website, mentioned again when they book, again a couple of weeks before the start and once more two days beforehand. One would think that this gives people enough time to prepare. Participants can give relatives or people who need to reach them the number of myself and my assistant, and we both check our phones hourly. So, there's really nothing that can go wrong on that front.

Quite clear, right? You cannot imagine the drama and resistance that goes on when they have to hand over their phones. It's as if I'm asking to give up their first-born child or their right leg! The first day is usually awkward as there's the habit to keep checking things but already on the second day the liberating feeling steps in. Not having to check anything. Not being so attached to a device. Realizing (again) how much time you actually have in a day. And, maybe most importantly, realizing how wonderful it is to have the majority of your daily sensory input be sounds, smells and stories of nature.

Input

As human Beings, we are tremendously influenced by what we consume every day. Our food intake can make us thrive or make us ill, as can the air we breathe, and the same goes for how we feed our minds.

Watching the news on a daily basis, maybe even more than once a day, is not purifying for the mind. News channels and newspapers know that our human mind is attracted by negativity and fear, so that is exactly what they feed us.

Mindlessly browsing time away on your phone, comparing yourself to other people (as that is basically what we are doing on social media) is not purifying for the mind. Binge watching, witnessing anything that involves deliberate violence, is not purifying for the mind.

Again, there is no yogic Principle Police to tell you that you can't do any of this. The only thing you can learn from the *Yoga Sutras* in this context is to become aware of what you do, and to check your energy levels. How do you feel after your free-time activity? Do you feel worthy to want the absolute best for yourself, to spend your free time on yourself?

When you are free to enjoy some relaxing time, who do you do this with?

Who are the people that you hang out with on a regular basis? Are they the kind of people who inspire you? Do they encourage you to pursue your dreams? Do they live their lives to their full potential? Do they value the same things as you do? Do you feel like you can be yourself with them?

Whether we like it or not, we are influenced by the people we surround ourselves with. They have an impact on our thinking, our behaviour, our self-esteem and our decisions. We could be the most grounded and positive person on the planet, but if we constantly surround ourselves with negative and fear-based people, they will hold us back.

Who do you hang out with?

If it's true that you become the average of the five people you spend the most time with, like Jim Rohn claimed, who are your five people? List them and evaluate if these are the right people for you right now. Do they match the person you want to be or become? Why or why not? If you need to make a change in this list, make the change.

Home

> Have nothing in your house that you do not know to be useful, or believe to be beautiful.
>
> *William Morris*

To state that a de-cluttered house will lead to a de-cluttered mind is bold, but I do know that it doesn't help to have a messy house when your mind is all over the place. Getting rid of stuff, as we saw in the previous chapter, doesn't mean that you can't have nice things in your house. It just means that you are conscious about buying new things. How were they made? Are they sustainable? Did anyone suffer to make them? As is mentioned in the quote above, is it useful? Are you actually using it? If not, get rid of it.

A house should be a place to re-energize, to feel at home. The mere feeling of being at home should give you some energy. Is that the case when you arrive home at the moment? Sometimes, it's as simple as having your house cleaned more often. I know it's a bit of a taboo to talk about, but some houses are just not clean enough. More clutter might make you lose the overview, and your keys. If your keys are always in the same place, however, you might just be buying time. It's a simple, stupid example but I also find it quite silly when people spend time looking for their keys. If you don't have to think about your keys, or anything else for that matter, imagine how much time you would save!

Not enough fresh air going through the house every day can also provoke a heavy energy in a home. The same goes for offices. I'm all in favour of windows that can be opened for fresh air and clean-desk theories; it's just so much easier to find your stuff, whether you want to have the 'nutty professor' image or not.

If you have a car, it's the same story. Why is your car a little (or a massive) dumpster? Keep it nice and clean and enjoy the ride!

Our planet, our home

This is not a new suggestion – you have probably read it before somewhere – so why aren't you doing it? Every single time that you go out into nature, whether it be the beach, a forest or the mountains, take a bag with you and fill it with garbage that you find. Really – every single time.

If we could all do that, across the globe, there would be less rubbish in our oceans, forests etc., and a lot more purity.

Mind bubble

Here's an experiment for you: imagine that the outside world could see your every thought. If you're a visual person like me, imagine that you have a giant screen above your head, like something digitally beamed or a cartoon bubble. Now, every single thought that comes into your head is automatically beamed up in real time, for everyone to see your thoughts. Live streaming at its best.

Think about that for a second. How would that impact your life and your relationships? Would you be in trouble with the people that you spend a lot of time with? Why? Relating back to the principle of purity, how pure are your thoughts on a daily basis? What are you thinking about? Are you concerned with what other people think of you? Or are you constantly distracted and not really listening to the people that you are with?

How conscious or aware are you when you are going through your day? And do you express what you're thinking and feeling? Why? If not, why not?

By simply imagining the thought screen or mind bubble for a couple of hours, actually thinking that it's there, how could that impact your day and your relationships?

Let's face it: you are disgusting

The result of the purity principle is explained in an interesting way in the *Yoga Sutras* and other scriptures. In some commentaries we can read: 'No matter how much perfume we put on, it only hides the dirt' (*Yoga Sutras*, translation and commentary by Sri Swami Satchidananda). Aren't you glad I'm translating these principles and ideas into modern life? I mean, just re-read that last sentence: 'it only hides the dirt'.

Why on earth would we want to feel disgust for our own bodies? However poetic it might sound to hide our own dirt, here we can clearly see that the principles were once again influenced by different ideologies, like Buddhism. In various Buddhist texts, we can read about how every minute some kind of impurity comes out of our exits. The idea is to develop a certain kind of indifference towards the body. And this links back to our previous principle of not being overly attached to our physical body, to no longer adore it or identify with it.

We can learn to have less of a fixation on our bodies and we can also stop being so obsessed with physical perfection, which gives us time, space and energy *to rest in peaceful awareness* with what is, with who we really are.

So we gain time, and that time we can use to study and learn more about the mind. Let's not forget to whom Patanjali was addressing his message: a predominantly male, ascetic crowd who dedicated their lives to the practice. Does this mean we can't use his teachings in today's world? Of course we can. If we see the body as *an accumulation of dirt* – another 'romantic' way of putting it – we become far less attracted and thus less obsessed with our own, or other, bodies which could potentially save us from a lot of *trouble*. The trouble we can avoid when we stop the struggle to desperately fight the signs of ageing, for example, and simply allow life to happen. By avoiding this trouble, when we start connecting with people beyond the physical, we're no longer focused on sexual or physical bodies. It's only then that we can become more aware of our inner body and our inner Self.

Psychological hygiene

The language that is used might be confusing; you could be reading this to mean that we should start neglecting our bodies, or should feel aversion to them. But this is not what the texts say.

A few years back, on a retreat in Wales, Alan Wallace told us a true story about the Dalai Lama, who once during a conference became all confused about certain words that the interpreter had used. At this point, in 1990, His Holiness didn't know the meaning of the words 'self-contempt' and 'self-hatred'. He asked his translator for an explanation, as these words don't exist in Tibetan. He almost cried when he discovered the meaning, as he couldn't believe there was such a feeling as self-hatred. When he found out that so many people actually feel this way about themselves, he had to take a moment to fully comprehend what he had just heard.

This example demonstrates that it's not aversion or self-hatred that we're looking for when discussing less attachment to the human body and mind, or about purifying it. When you identify with your body, with your thoughts, you are setting yourself up for disaster if your thoughts are very negative. But, when you can sense that the thoughts are there *for you*, that might make a situation a lot lighter. *Thoughts are at my service and I'm happy to take great care of them and use them* – welcome to the practice of concentration and meditation.

> If you don't use your human mind, don't expect to get another one.
>
> *Attributed to H.H. the Dalai Lama*

Some people tell me that they can't meditate because they are different to other people. They are always thinking, always busy and thus it's impossible for them to not think and to calm their mind. It's probably because they are creative, smart, solution-focused – they will use whatever other good-sounding, ego-boosting adjective to point out that they don't want to meditate.

I know exactly what they are talking about because I also have a wicked, rebellious, creative and beautiful mind of my own. The difference is that I am constantly training my mind, and they don't want to. The 'I cannot' should really be replaced by 'I don't want to' because anyone can meditate.

Let's meditate

So, how do you start or restart with a meditation practice to purify the mind? You have probably noticed that in this book I usually put concentration and meditation next to each other, as what most people call meditation is actually a form of concentration. You can focus or concentrate on your breathing, on a mantra, on a candle and so on. When the mind quietens down after a while through this concentration, it is only then that the actual meditation can start.

In Chapter 4, we examined a technique to break free from mindlessly continuing with bad habits: pause, relax, reflect and choose an action. Setting off a meditation practice is quite similar.

Step 1: pause

Pausing is the first step, translated into *making the time* to train the mind.

Step 2: relax

The second step is to start relaxing. If you're hyper-tense, it's just unfair towards yourself to expect to be able to instantly concentrate on something. That's why we often hear that we should take a couple of deep breaths first. Is it that simple? Well, yes. Give it a try, right here, right now. Take three nice, long, deep breaths, please.

Let's be honest, if taking three nice, long, deep breaths right here, right now is too much to ask, you really don't want to strive for a better world. Why? Well, you clearly don't want to put in the effort to have exceptional mental health and mental wellbeing, which will enable you to react more appropriately towards other people; it would be for your benefit as well as others' that you would do the work. You would be able to choose your reactions wisely instead of mindlessly reacting, because you have created an undercurrent of peace of mind.

Are you serious about unlocking your true potential? Then breathe deeply three times, right now, and afterwards keep reading to explore this topic a little more.

What should you do if you don't like what I wrote above and you're not ready to make the effort? Not to worry, you can still smile; it doesn't mean instant death and destruction. There is hope. For now, just let go of the whole idea of meditating and move on to the next chapter. Just be patient. Maybe, one day, you will want to check this part of the book again. Maybe not. It's all good. The only thing I wish for you is to be more peaceful and relaxed, with or without meditation.

Becoming a softie

There's a misconception about meditation that I would like to clarify, and that's the idea that you become soft, lethargic, slow and rather dull when you meditate. I have no idea where that comes from, but I just know that we can become more passionate and intense than ever before, with a relaxed mind as an undercurrent. Actually, we become sharper and much more attentive when we are relaxed. The mind can focus so much better; it's more creative and laser-sharp. Just because we have trained the mind to keep that single pointed attention and focus for a long time. So we see things clearer. Because the mind doesn't wander off so much. We enhance our clarity so much more when the mind is relaxed and stable.

Now that we have some misconceptions out of the way, let's check the next step!

Step 3: observe

Once you have found that tiny bit more relaxation, you can move on and start observing your reality. Simply listen to what you can hear and become deeply still, observing if there are many thoughts, or not so many.

And finally, observe your breathing. You don't have to change anything about your breathing, just observe. As if this was the very first time you became aware of your breathing.

You check what is moving when you inhale; you zoom in on what's moving in your body when you exhale. And you keep doing this for a while, while trying not to interfere with the breathing.

Step 4: concentrate

Your next step to mastering meditation is to start concentrating. As you were already becoming more aware of your breathing, counting your breaths in rounds of ten works really well for most people. Every combo of an inhale and an exhale is one count. The next inhale/exhale is another count, and so on.

Step 5: release

While you are counting your breaths, many thoughts will be coming by. Instead of being frustrated or giving in to all kinds of unnecessary mental comments about being unfit for meditation, be happy! Yes, be happy as you have a good functioning brain that produces thoughts! This means that you are intelligent and creative! *Olé!*

The trick is not to get caught in any of the thoughts. You see or hear the thoughts, recognize that they are there, but you do not focus on anything. My own reaction to thoughts used to be the following sentence: *Oh, how interesting that this comes up, what else is there?* Again, and again, and again.

At a certain point, you can stop counting and focus only on the breaths. You keep following one breath and only one breath. Every single breath is different and therefore a breath can never be boring.

After your timer goes off, just relax again for a couple of breaths and continue your day.

The actual concentration/meditation process is a continuous cycle of five steps: pausing, relaxing, observing, concentrating and releasing. Unfortunately, you will not find depth or insight after only a couple of meditation sessions; training the mind takes a bit of time. And *a bit* is quite an understatement. But the results of having a more balanced and healthier mind are so beneficial for yourself and others that I can only encourage you to give it a try! I must add that this is just one technique of meditation that I'm mentioning here; there are many more. Over time, though, I have noticed that this technique is an easy one to grasp and remember for most people.

Despite all the good intentions, getting yourself to start meditating can still be a bit of a struggle. In my experience, most people think they need to give something up in order to meditate, and all kinds of *rebellious* thoughts make us bail out. One single sentence has helped me to stick to my practice: *I do not negotiate.*

I do not negotiate!

This has been one of my personal mantras when it comes to meditation. A long time ago, I made a vow: to meditate every day. I realized what the benefits could be, had been meditating on and off for years and I was ready for more depth. So, the plan was to start every single morning with 24 minutes of mindful breathing.

Knowing myself and my inner rebel, who instantly needs to resist any kind of firm rule or compliance (remember our purple goat?), I came to terms with myself that this new habit wasn't negotiable. I would just do it for a while and evaluate later. The simple fact that there was no room for negotiation, even when tired, when rushed, when not in the mood, made me stick with it. There was no room to postpone the meditation to the evening. There was no reason to moan as I had 'agreed' to do this. Years later, I still don't negotiate my morning routine.

It was only after using this mantra for a couple of years that I came to know that this sentence might just as well be in the *Yoga Sutras*, it being linked in the commentaries to our sixth principle of purity and the act of training our minds.

In his commentary, Sri Swami Satchidananda teaches us that *when we take a vow, we should stick to it*. This is also linked to the principle of self-discipline, which we will explore further in Chapter 8. Right now, I would like to share the following, which you might relate to (I sure did).

> The moment we decide to fast, a friend will bring us something delicious to eat. It makes us feel very sad. Just today I decided to fast. She could have brought this cake over yesterday. Hmm. I think I'll just postpone my fast until tomorrow. In this way, we fail our exam. When we take a vow, we should stick to it. There will be ample tests to tempt us to break it.
>
> *Sri Swami Satchidananda*

Connection fail: meet the SPOB

One of the definitions of Yoga is 'union', which is ultimately what we all strive for – more connection with ourselves, more union with the people we love, with the people we work with, and maybe even with strangers.

Cultivating a more balanced mind takes time, which is something you have. It's like going to the gym when you're overweight and feeling you don't fit in. A six-hour workout will not make you look good. But working out six times a week for 20 minutes a day will definitely make a difference after three months.

We live in a fast-paced society, and we demand results fast – 24/7. I get it, *if you want something, you want it now.*

In a way, when we act like that we are no more than little spoilt brats who can't make the effort needed to get some real and lasting results.

You don't want to be a SPOiled Brat, do you? I don't know about you, but I would rather not be called a spoiled brat. It's quite offensive, and that is why I have now made it into 'SPOB', to remind us all. I don't want to be a SPOB; do you?

If we behave like SPOBs, it will be very difficult to connect to people, to find that union. Who wants to hang out with a SPOB? The same goes for having not-so-pure thoughts about other people. It simply interferes with the free flow of easy and natural connection.

Worker in, victim out

What most people don't get is that cultivating a more balanced mind takes time. And we have the time.

Lots of people constantly see different specialists, follow different therapies or yet another physical coach, psychologist, dietician, reiki person, turning to all kinds of people to fix their problems. However, nothing will get fixed for real if *you* don't do the work. There will be days that getting, being and staying on the cushion will be really hard. There will be days when working out is almost undoable. And still. Nobody else can fix our own mental issues as such. We need to go through it all and do the work.

Stop playing the victim and placing the responsibility for more peace of mind in somebody else's hands. It's under your own control to do the work, or not. Sometimes it takes a long time to find some more peace of mind and mental wellbeing. And, for sure, sometimes we might need professional help to show us the way, but at least we can put in the effort.

Just relax, keep doing the work, keep going, step by step. If you continue, no doubt that there will be times when you feel more at ease, calmer and more confident, which leads to a state of more contentment, our next chapter and principle.

Change-maker: if you could see what I'm thinking right now...

Today, throughout your entire day, imagine that you have the mind bubble-screen above you. The screen described above is beaming out your every thought.

A scary idea, perhaps, but imagine it today so you can become more aware of your thought process. Reflect: does this thought bring me something good or will it make somebody's heart sing? Can I qualify this as a purifying thought or is it doing any harm?

Change-maker: compassion walk

I first heard about this idea through Sri Sri Ravi Shankar so I will use his words here.

Make some time to go for a walk and during this walk, you make a conscious effort to see everyone, regardless of their behaviour, as doing the best they can in that moment. Instead of making any judgements, try assuming they are struggling in the same ways you are, and send a silent prayer for them to suffer less, to have opportunities to learn and grow.

This is a great way to develop a non-judgemental attitude towards all, and to foster emotional purity and stability.

7

CONTENTMENT

Checking the *Yoga Sutras* and the Sanskrit language, we derive our next principle of contentment, or *santosha*, from the words *san*, meaning 'entirely', and *tosha*, meaning 'acceptance'. This can potentially result in two translations, namely 'satisfaction' and 'contentment'.

These are very different words with a different meaning in English, so this seemingly clear concept can actually confuse us. According to Patanjali, cultivating a feeling of contentment is crucial to our development process. He even states that it's impossible to be dissatisfied with oneself, or with anything else in life, and still fully reach our highest potential.

So, before we dive in any further, let's first tackle the difference between satisfaction and contentment. When you feel satisfied, this means that there was a desire or a need that is now satisfied, so at the moment you no longer have that need or desire. Satisfaction is conditional. *If I get this, then I will be satisfied.* And you will be satisfied, until the next desire pops up.

When you feel content, this means that you completely accept 'what is' and not what you think *reality should be*. This leads us to saying that you can be very content and at the same time not necessarily satisfied. Reality as you perceive it may not have worked out the way you had envisioned it, expectations might not have been met, but you still feel content.

While I am writing this, I have been on several trains for the past six hours; I have another two hours to go and I'm *somewhere* in the middle of Germany. The train conductor just checked my ticket and made a bit of a thing because I'm on the 'wrong' train as I could have taken four earlier and faster trains. *Eh, yes, my dear man, I would have if every single one of those trains had not been either delayed or cancelled.* My expectation was that the entire trip would only take five hours (not eight) and I would change trains twice, but the German railways decided differently and made me detour and change trains five times. Am I satisfied with how this trip is going? Not really. I would have preferred to spend more time with the person who's picking me up at the station and I can't wait to see him. Am I content? Absolutely; a delay will not mess up the naturally good feeling that I have right now.

The ego says, the spirit says, Rachel says

The ego says: 'Once everything falls into place, I will find peace,' This is the satisfaction approach.

The spirit says: 'Find peace and everything will fall into place.' This is the contentment approach.

It's not only the 'spirit' telling you this. The *Yoga Sutras* and I are telling you this too. Literature is divided about who wrote these lines first, but I have been sharing them for years now as they are so profound. Two very simple lines of text, and yet they are so powerful. They are here for you, to read and re-read.

Being content

Contentment doesn't mean that you are leaning on the illusion that life is what it is and nothing can be changed. It's all about how to bring more meaning to your life, and to the lives of others.

If your life already feels meaningful, the question is: *what can I bring to this party called life, instead of what I can get out of it?* It's cultivating an attitude of being alright with whatever is. Accept whatever is and take this moment as your starting point for change. You don't disapprove of anything that is occurring; you don't fight it or rebel against it. It just is.

Most people realize that there's no point in jumping up and down, completely frustrated, because it's raining but you wished for sunshine. But, funnily enough, most people don't realize that jumping up and down and feeling completely frustrated when life doesn't unfold the way you planned makes as little sense as raging over the weather.

You find yourself in an unexpected traffic jam; people are unfriendly to you; your flight is delayed; you didn't get the promotion; everyone around you is annoying; the whole world is turned upside down because of a virus; you got sick... How do you react when these kinds of things happen?

The attitude of acceptance, for sure, points towards the physical as well. We touched upon this subject very briefly in Chapter 1, as non-violence and contentment go hand-in-hand in this context. Maybe you have an injured shoulder or knee. It's far from convenient and really limits you in sports. These kinds of situations are glorious moments to practise contentment, because naturally, at first, you will be far from content about the injury. At the same time, accepting the injury, taking care of it in the kindest way, will be the crucial step in going forward. Some things might never really heal but you can find a way to work with existing injuries.

Emo-bumper

You may be aware that certain things (like being overweight) no longer serve you. If we follow what I wrote above, we can commit to change, as soon as we accept the current situation.

This is easier said than done. I know, because so many people in my coaching sessions and retreats struggle with this idea, so I will focus on this a little bit more.

Usually women, but more and more men as well, develop what we call 'an emotional bumper' around the waist. A bit of extra fat that seems to be quite stuck, and it's the very last part that disappears when you go on a diet. Besides manic exercise, lifestyle change, cardio and a decent diet (yes, only those four...), quite often a breakthrough question to losing the extra weight is: what are you protecting yourself from?

At some point in time, it was perhaps needed to brace yourself due to certain circumstances. You needed a bit of *reserve* to be able to cope with a situation. Abusive relationships, a job where the life/work balance is totally out-of-whack, caretaking – all examples where there's both a physical and an emotional drain. Being aware of your present situation, trusting that it's safe to let go of the bumper and thus the past, can really kick off that 'miraculous' weight loss.

And this is exactly why contentment comes before self-discipline as a Yoga principle. We need to fully accept what is before we can change it. And this also explains why non-violence is the very first principle, as everything needs to be seen in the light of non-violence. All principles fit wonderfully together when you *take* a moment to think about it.

It is what it is

Most people dive into something new and push forward solely on willpower and self-discipline, completely leaving out the contentment element, as they believe they will be content *once* this or that condition is fulfilled. *I will be content as soon as I lose ten pounds. I will be content when I find someone who loves me.* In other words, there are conditions to your contentment and that can never work.

In today's world, you probably hear more than ever the sentence 'life is what it is and we need to accept life as it is'. In most cases, this sentence gives me the chills as it's just another brilliant way to spiritually bypass just about anything. I've talked about it already in the chapter on non-attachment. It's nothing but an excuse to justify laziness, unwillingness to act upon a given situation or giving up on something. It gives you a freebie to stay away from change and perhaps even from following up on a dream.

So how to go forward?

Step 1 is to accept the current situation and ideally even see how it all served you up until this point. When you then commit (step 2) to different habits and follow through (step 3) because you know why, there is no doubt that you will succeed.

When you follow these steps, the entire concept of struggle simply falls out of the equation. There is no struggle as such. You will eat healthily because you want to. There is no longing for food that makes you feel bad afterwards. You exercise because you want to take care of your body and it's no longer an effort.

And that is what gives you the *joy*. The joy of raising the standard, bringing as much value as you can to your life and the lives of others.

The result of being content is joy

'The main purpose of life is joy' – I have heard the Dalai Lama say it, and Patanjali also tells us that contentment brings unsurpassed joy! Feelings of happiness, joy, love and appreciation are natural and so easy to feel. Once we achieve a balanced mind, we need to uncover what is obscuring our sight, so we can feel again what is natural.

We can undermine our impulsive reactivity to anything that comes up, anything we see, becoming more aware, more present of what is going on, at a deeper level. Don't always question *why* this or that is happening to you. It only causes more suffering.

Bluhh...

In Chapter 5, we identified the modern definition of 'success' as *having a lot of stuff*. If we reframe the standard of success to the amount of joy we feel, a whole new world opens up – it is not simply how much we consume, or how much we achieve.

In my coaching practice, I encounter people who have achieved all they wanted to achieve for themselves: family life, more than enough money, a great body, great friends, awesome holidays, cool hobbies and still... there's this overall feeling of 'bluhh'...

There is no joy; everything has just become very serious and, typically, they have nobody who inspires them. They have forgotten to have fun, to be silly and joke because they have been working so hard to reach what they now have.

We are constantly running after beauty, power, money, fame, strength, knowledge and, once we have it, we think that contentment will follow. Instead of wanting peace, contentment, control of our egos, fun and love, we focus on all that is outside of ourselves. We really need to turn things around as this is the only way we can ever start manifesting. It's not about what we want and will get in a materialistic way – this approach will never bring us what we really want.

What matters

Chasing money is often something you do because, underneath, you want to be recognized and loved by others. What is usually missing is the sense of making a difference. The danger in today's society is in being so busy chasing goals and succeeding that you completely 'forget' about others – even when people claim that they work hard *for* the family, so they won't lack anything financially. *They can buy and do whatever they want!* The problem with this is that the real contribution, other than financial wellbeing, is minimal. It's about contributing with your love and attention to the people you love the most first, and then expanding it to universal love and contribution.

No, we don't need to all start a fund or sponsor a children's hospital somewhere. (Well, if you have the money, please do sponsor a good cause.) But, starting a hospital or a charity is like starting a new business; it's exciting, it's a challenge, you can put your name on it, you'll get recognition, it is a lot of fun… for you. Again, for you. When I talk about contribution, this is not what I mean.

You also contribute when you are nice to other people on a daily basis, to the first person you see on the street, to the person serving you a meal in a restaurant.

You also contribute when you are aware of your purchases, glass or plastic; are they good or bad for the planet?

You also contribute when you are honest, when you do not lie. Especially not to the people you love, or who trust you.

You also contribute when you choose love over 'being right'. It's that simple. That is very different to donating loads of money, especially if money doesn't mean that much to you, or if you have enough anyway that the donation will hardly leave a dent. Can't it be a win-

win situation? Isn't there always an egocentric aspect in charity?

There is no wrong or right answer.

My only wish is for you to feel better, happier and more content. So in this light, if you're feeling that despite having *everything* there is something lacking in your life, maybe you can check the kind of contribution that you are giving to the world, and to the people around you.

Who's got the bigger one?

Besides longing for the next thing, and feeling satisfaction upon obtaining it, and thus your happiness level depending on fulfilling your needs and desires, comparison is also an excellent way to set you up for tragedy.

Just one question here: do you often compare yourself to others?

Be here now

Contentment means to be alright with what is and to be fully present, at all times. In Chapter 3 on non-stealing, I asked you if you were still here or whether your mind was halfway somewhere else. Well, the next concept is very similar.

This has been and still is something I need to work on myself, as my mind loves planning. Let me rephrase that: my mind is obsessed with planning. When I started meditating, a long time ago, I was advised to keep a journal and note down the things that came up during my attempts to train the mind. There was one single word that came up the most: *Planning. Planning. Planning, planning and more planning!*

I can be in the most amazing environment and my mind suddenly goes into planning mode. It made me efficient as an operational director and it makes me plan the retreats in detail, having plan A, B, C and D ready. But this also means that I really have to remind myself to not plan *all* the time. I come to a new place and instantly my mind starts: *oh wow, this could be an excellent place for a retreat. What could we do here, who would like to cook here? What kinds of excursions can we do?* As I am writing this book, halfway through it, I am already planning the next one... Future achievements, adventures; it goes on and on and on.

It's also about running on the beach and coming up with marketing ideas to promote your business. When you do all this while running on a beach, you tend to forget how magical and beautiful it is! This is not contentment. That is not 'being awake'. This is almost the opposite of what the Buddha was trying to teach us: to be awake and fully aware of every single moment.

We train the mind so that we are able to return to the present moment, give it our full attention, and keep the planning mind for times when we can and do need to plan. It's only when we focus on the running that the real satisfaction and contentment of the act, of the environment, of the people we are with can occur: that is contentment. And like so many things we identify with, it's a habit, a behaviour we display. It's not who we really are; it's a choice we make to act like that, or not.

Yes, but I like to be busy and running is ideal to think about those things. If I didn't do that, be like that, push myself like that, I wouldn't reach my goals. Again, there is no Principle Police, so you can do whatever you like!

My question is: have you tried a different approach? What I'm referring to is that there is a place and time for everything. We have time to work, to be creative, to write down our goals, to focus. And then there are times when we can relax.

Some people, some minds tend to never relax, always running after the next thing. As long as they can keep busy with all kinds of things, they don't need to look inside. This is very practical: there is no time to look inside so they can't look into the sadness, the darkness, the grief, the restlessness, the signs the body is telling them.

Gratitude 2.0

We sometimes forget gratitude; that's why I repeat it, again and again. In the fast-paced and instant world we live in, the forgetting actually makes perfect sense. We're frustrated when we can't find a flight with convenient flight hours. We get snappy when there's a traffic jam. And this is just traffic issues.

Being a Yoga teacher doesn't free you from these kinds of day-to-day frustrations. Just recently, I was looking for a flight to Belgium, agitated, as the whole reason for going would be to solve some kind of an administrative mix-up. It meant travel, time, hassle and money, and as far as I could understand it was all purely due to bureaucracy. *My holy persona* just forgot about one thing, and that is the absence of feeling any gratitude for the whole situation, not even thinking about how lucky I am that I can fly over to another continent in the blink of an eye.

Swipe the card and done, we're off. I clearly have enough money, time, health and the right documents to do so. Living in a country like Morocco, where the vast majority of Moroccans will never have the opportunity to fly to Europe, something started dawning on me. I felt a short moment of shame; it was quite humbling – although I know there's no need for shame as this is a feeling that doesn't serve anyone. Gratitude and toning down the frustration levels was much more effective.

Of course, the minute that I totally accepted the situation, I found a flight and did a short meditation on gratefulness, and what happened? The whole situation solved itself.

Change frustration for instant appreciation and watch the magic unfold. You need to mean it, though. Not just words; take the time to feel it. Both the frustration and the gratitude. Once again, that is why we need to be aware, to be conscious of our thoughts, behaviour and actions; that is why we want to *be awake*.

Mind-stuff

Being awake can mean relaxing the brain that is constantly thinking about survival and competition. It means to stop comparing yourself to others. Relaxing the constant urge to push forward and reach goals without being content with what is. Having goals and aspirations, heck yes! But we must also be content with what we have now, and enjoy what we have already achieved.

There is joy in whatever it is that you have already achieved. To just be with yourself and connect, relax and enjoy your own company. You have made it this far. Things worked out, didn't they? You're able to read this book so things have worked out; maybe they were not easy – gosh no, far from easy – but you can sit down and read this book. This mere fact holds the potential for gratefulness.

Remember, pure joy comes naturally from contentment, but without contentment, even if it's still possible, it will be far more difficult to experience true joy.

Connection fail: it's not enough

One of the definitions of Yoga is 'union', which is ultimately what we all strive for – more connection with ourselves, more union with the people we love, with the people we work with, and maybe even with strangers.

More union is not possible when we want what's not ours, steal what's not ours. If you are truly content, you won't have a tendency to take what isn't yours or cling on to things that you need to let go of. This means you can let go of people and things more easily and you create an opportunity for more union and less separation. When you are content with what is, you will have an antidote for expectations taking over control.

Practising contentment will lead us to a lighter view on life, and will make it so much easier to accept life as it is. Not just as a spiritually bypassing answer, but as something that we can actually use in our daily life.

If there's only one thing you remember from this chapter, I suggest the paradox that was given earlier: *it is when we accept what is that we can start the change.* It's at that moment that we can tap into self-discipline to follow through with our idea of change, the topic of our next chapter.

Change-maker: go and be content!

En*joy* the rest of the day. Be fully present and en*joy*; do whatever makes you content. And *be* in the moment. Yes, that might sound a bit woo-hoo, spiritual and all that, but still – I invite you to just do it.

The key is in the practice. Practice will make us aware that we know. The awakened mind is the natural mind. But that means we need to dive in and explore.

Change-maker: yes please; thank you

Please have in mind what it is in your life right now that is causing you a feeling of dissatisfaction. This can be something related to your job, relationship, body, home… Put into words what it is exactly that is causing the feeling of dissatisfaction.

Below, I will give the relationship example, as many people will be able to relate to it, but you can replace this with whatever is holding you back from jumping with joy right now.

I would like to have a romantic relationship. Is it possible for you to see that there were many events leading up to the current situation? *I didn't allow anyone in my life because I was too scared to get hurt again. No dating, not even trying, avoiding places where I could meet someone, running whenever it could get serious…*

Is it possible for you to see that this situation, however bizarre it might be, has actually served you, up until this point? *It gave me peace of mind, in a way, as I could do my own thing, focus on my job, build a career, date lots of people without any strings attached, investigate my needs in a relationship, have times with lots of sex, times with no need to have sex at all...*

Is it possible to start from a feeling of contentment about this situation, accepting it fully and then start taking action towards the desired situation? It's only when you fully accept the current situation that things can start to change. A positive affirmation like the one below could help you to change your behaviour. Every time you go on autopilot and want to run when meeting someone you like, think of these lines and stay.

It has served me to be single and I'm very grateful for this time. At this point, being single doesn't serve me any longer and I'm very happy to open up again, to let love in. The right relationship for me is just around the corner; I'm ready for it and I can feel the love.

8

SELF-DISCIPLINE

Traditionally, the term *tapas* referred to the fire at the centre of a ritual. Over time, it morphed into a more subtle meaning of austerity, concentrated discipline, penance or heat. And in the *Yoga Sutras*, it took the meaning of staying in the tension of opposites. Eventually, we began to boil it down to self-discipline, or taking your power back.

Some people have a bit too much; some people could use a bit more. My years of practice have convinced me that self-discipline is one of the keys to living a light and joyful life. When we practise it, we can create new patterns for our body, mind and speech.

It's the cultivation of self-discipline that allows us to be present in the here-and-now with whatever is occurring, whether it be positive, negative or neutral. I often mention these words in guided meditations when we observe our thoughts. Our thoughts can be pleasant, unpleasant or neutral; whatever they may be, we stay and observe.

If you see willpower as a battery, it makes total sense that sometimes we run out of power. When you have too many goals to accomplish, there's simply no energy left at the end of the day to 'be good' all the way.

Let me give you an example of what daily life might look like. When it takes you a good deal of effort just to get out of bed in the morning to meditate for 20 minutes, you have used up quite a bit of your willpower battery already, before breakfast. When you then meet your commitment to eat healthily by making a good breakfast and taking your homemade lunch with you to work, this uses another big chunk of your willpower battery.

Add to that a firm commitment to work hard at your job, and maybe even to go to the gym or a Yoga class after work. By the time you come home, you could be in a bit of a pickle; there is just enough energy left to take care of your family and call your mom but simply nothing else left to take care of yourself, let alone to do something really rejuvenating in the evening. And you think, *but I did so well, all day*. Failing at the end here makes perfect sense if you see willpower and self-discipline as a battery.

We'll discuss how your belief system, habits and thoughts influence this process in both a positive and negative manner later in this chapter, but the idea of a 'willpower battery' gives us a nice insight into why we sometimes fail at the end of the day.

Kindness rating

I deliberately use the phrase 'be good', as this is the criterion by which quite a few people judge themselves. We wonder, 'Have I been good today with my diet and exercises?' We hardly ever judge ourselves on our compassion or kindness success rate. We hardly ever evaluate who received our full attention, or if we were aware of our conversation tone in that meeting. Instead of wondering whether we've 'been good', we could ask ourselves: *did I take into account the kind of energy I was giving? Was I aware of other people's needs?*

External self-discipline

Let's check first why we would need self-discipline – and what for – in body, mind and speech. There are two types of discipline: internal and external. Internal discipline is our self-restraint. External discipline is according to social norms, such as following the law or rules in sports. We simply need self-discipline in sports; it's the fundamental basis on which sports have been created. Every player must adhere to the rules of the game, and in order to achieve results and finish our trainings, we need to push ourselves to reach our goals.

'I am not a runner' – or at least that's what I had said enough times to myself to believe it. I started a couple of times 20 years ago and I really didn't like it. My stomach got all upset and I blamed this on years of taking overloads of migraine medications, leading to a missing gallbladder, kidney and liver issues etc. These were nothing but wonderful excuses, as objectively none of these issues makes you unable to run.

One day in Essaouira, I met Alice Morrison, who invited me to jog along with her on the beach. I found myself saying yes. It sounded like a really nice thing to do and it fitted in with my plan, as I had made the resolution to be fitter than ever this year. Little did I know then that Alice had run the *Marathon des Sables*! This is a 250-kilometre ultra-race comprising six marathons in six days, in the Moroccan Sahara! Every time I would ask Alice whether I should build things up or have running schemes, she would simply answer: 'Oh c'mon, Rachel, just run.' And so I did. My stomach got seriously upset on our first runs, storming into all kinds of very unnecessary fight-or-flight actions, and I would frequently try to remind myself that I'm not a runner. But I just kept following her, step after step, mile after mile.

Whether I really should have built up to it or not is beside the point, because what stuck were her words: 'Oh c'mon, Rachel, just run.' Because I knew exactly why I wanted to run – I wanted to be fitter than ever this year – I got on with it. Repeating these words didn't make running easy, but they surely made it a lot easier.

A compelling reason to run and a mantra to keep me going when things started to become difficult were all I needed to have the self-discipline to keep running.

Internal discipline and the monkey mind

Whether you see Yoga classes as sports or not, the practice of holding a posture has everything to do with self-discipline. In some lessons, I have students stay in a position a lot longer than the usual five to ten breaths. The immediate response is that they want to get out of the position. But sometimes the magic of experiencing awareness and mindfulness in class only happens when we stay – when we don't move. (Unless there is a sharp pain in the back, neck, knees or hips, of course.) To explore this, I advise students to practise with a qualified teacher to help identify that fine line between discomfort and pain.

Self-discipline holds the key to calming our distracted minds. Buddhism describes the mind as being filled with monkeys, hence the term 'monkey mind'. These monkeys swing from one branch of thought to the next, wanting the next banana, the next big thing, the next small thing. Always wanting something. Monkey minds love multitasking: worrying, planning and dreaming, all at the same time. They like to be mindless. When we develop self-discipline, the heat of our fire consumes the distractions of the monkey mind so it can be focused and mindful. The self-discipline burns distractions so our minds can purify. Such acceptance makes the mind strong and steady.

Verbal self-discipline

A smart leader knows when to hold his tongue and when to speak, showing us how self-discipline can greatly influence our speech. Discipline helps us in building a sense of self-control that enables us to be silent or to speak up.

It requires great self-discipline to not spread our opinion in a discussion or on a broader platform. To practise self-discipline throughout our lives, we must constantly ask ourselves: will people benefit more by hearing another opinion, or do they need to see our actions? On the other hand, it also requires great inner strength at times to speak our truth. For more on this – because, once again, all of these principles are linked – check Chapter 2 on truthfulness.

Many students on my retreats are relatively new to Yoga. After a week of relaxation and feeling the effects of a Yoga practice, they get all excited and blissed out and they want the whole world to start practising Yoga. 'Oh, if only my friend, sister, brother, boss, colleague, mom would do this. You know what? I will buy them a retreat', they say. If the people in their lives are completely new to Yoga, I will probably advise against this gift, because what arouses people's interest is not being told how *they* can change, but rather the process of seeing *someone else* change. They can see how we glow, how our speech and actions are different. I encourage my enthusiastic students to let their friends and family ask about what has brought on this transformation. Then, of course, we can promote the practice and mention how utterly awesome it is to go on a retreat. Restricting the desire to share our opinion about Yoga, therefore, can be an act of willpower.

Pitfalls to self-discipline

Let's check the things that can undermine our ability to reach our goals. While this chapter is focused on cultivating self-discipline, I'm not recommending that you follow blind ambition and become a fully disciplined person overnight. Many of us set unattainable goals for ourselves – and then, when we make a mistake in our new routine, on day two or week two or month two, we give up. We can't force ourselves to become perfectly disciplined overnight, so expect some failure to happen along the way! Failure is not necessarily bad; it just means we realize that we slipped. And we will slip. Just know that one step off the track won't derail your master plan from success. And sometimes, we haven't been completely honest in our goal-setting. There is absolutely nothing wrong with re-evaluating our goals every now and then.

Too often, I hear that people feel 'they've fallen off the wagon' and can't get back up because they have failed so badly that they are back to square one. The good thing is that we can never really go back to square one because we are constantly changing. If you ever feel like this, know that the discipline you have shown in the past is not lost. You can pick it up again at any point in time.

What holds us back is fear. When it comes to potential pitfalls to self-discipline, fear is probably the most important factor that keeps us from getting the results we want. Why do most of us not meditate every single day, for example? We all know it's good for us. Why is it that one of the first things we do when we get too busy is to drop exercise, Yoga and meditation?

You may have heard this Zen proverb: 'You need to meditate 20 minutes per day, unless you are busy; in that case, meditate for at least an hour.' We drop the things we know are good for us because there is 'something way stronger' that outweighs the possible long-term effects of meditation and sports. I suggest that in many cases, this 'stronger thing' is rooted in fear.

The fear of 'peeling' off our outer layers when meditating and not knowing what we'll find underneath is one example of this. Many of us harbour a fear of not knowing what is going to happen. Students ask me, 'You keep saying that we all are brilliant diamonds on the inside, Rachel, but what if there is nothing inside me? What if I am just an empty box?' I have heard this so many times from successful, self-assured and beautiful people. Of course, this will hold us back in our meditation. Of course, it's so much more interesting to keep ourselves busy with a million things 'to do' instead of sitting down and being quiet. I firmly believe that everyone has that massive diamond inside that's just waiting to shine (again). That's the whole reasoning behind the naming of my company – revealing the diamond within, Revealing Vajra, as one of the meanings of *vajra* is 'diamond'.

First and foremost, we need to trust that what is inside us is a brilliant, bright, shiny diamond and that we are worthy of the lives we are living. *I am totally awesome and I am totally worthy of being here!* This should be a mantra to shout out loud, but most people I tell it to just give me a shy grin.

We may be holding on to an underlying feeling that what we do is not enough, that it's insignificant or unimportant and that we need to serve a bigger goal. We tend to trivialize our roles as mothers or fathers, or our professional roles at work. We might think that we need to save the planet and change the world – that people have expectations and high demands of us that we will never be able to live up to. But the antidote to all that comes down to trusting that who we are is quite enough. When we are authentic and loving, starting with the people around us, we are enough. This brings us back to the first principle of non-violence and cosmic love. What if 'enough' simply means influencing the people around us by showing our actions and our Being, and letting everyone simply be themselves?

The enemies of self-discipline are laziness, lethargy and procrastination. These factors can definitely hold us back from reaching our goals. This is when we have the energy to do things but we don't really want to. When evaluating this, let's not forget our battery metaphor and consider that perhaps we're not merely lazy at the end of the day, but rather that there's just no energy left any more.

A lack of clear motivation is another factor that can hold us back from showing self-discipline and reaching our goals. When asked what makes them great, many world champions in business and sports tend to give similar answers: 'I had a vision'; 'I saw my future'; 'I had a dream'. We need this type of clear motivation to cultivate self-discipline.

Knowing why we want to reach certain goals is crucial for our success. Whether it is to learn a new skill, reach a sports goal, achieve a mental goal, learn a new language or stop a specific habit, we need to have a compelling reason in order to follow through. Sometimes we need to correct our intentions regarding why we are doing the things that we are doing on a daily basis – perhaps even several times a day.

Self-discipline is needed from the minute we open our eyes in the morning until the minute we close them at night. Every time we notice that we are having thoughts that do not serve us, we need self-discipline to turn them into different thoughts. We need self-discipline to get up a little bit earlier in the morning to exercise. We need to remain friendly when others might not be, to be focused and laser-sharp at work. We need self-discipline to consciously choose to maintain a healthy diet, to keep ourselves from taking that extra piece of cake.

The entire day is full of *must*s and *to-do*s. If, in the evening, there's consistently nothing left in your willpower battery, you might want to re-check what was said in Chapter 4 about energy management and how to recharge. If you lack the motivation to perform certain tasks that you know are good for you, there are a few things that you need to look at first. For example, when looking back, what has enabled you to get things done in the past? Are you the kind of person who thrives with a disciplined action routine or does fired-up motivation get you to move forward? For some, motivation through knowing the outcome is enough of a kick. For others, having a set and definitive routine is the right way to go.

Countering distraction and rebellion

Distraction might be one of the toughest things to counter these days. The average American adult (18+) spends over four hours on their smartphone every day, and it's said that millennials check their phones about 150 times per day.

According to the late Michael Stone: 'We are living in an attention-deficit society caught between passive laxity on the one hand and hyperactivity on the other.' We need techniques to re-establish our attention, so we can re-learn how to fully relax.

Wikipedia tells us that 'Self-discipline can be defined as the ability to motivate oneself in spite of a negative emotional state'. You may have rolled your eyes at the beginning of this chapter if you associate the idea of self-discipline with self-denial, limitation, pain, scarcity and lack. I get it. Most people simply don't like rules and regulations – myself included! If someone tells me that I *have to* do something, my inner eight-year-old rebel is instantly triggered and my initial intention will be to do the exact opposite – purple goat alert!

This was one of the main reasons why I kept postponing doing a *vipassana* retreat. Nowadays, it seems to be a thing to 'do *vipassana*' just like you 'do Yoga' but when it was introduced to me, all I knew about the ten-day silent *vipassana* retreat was the strict rules involved. I heard that *vipassana* wasn't just about being silent and not communicating verbally; there were rules for showering, eating and even specifics on where and how to walk. Because I didn't know the reasons behind these rules, and I didn't investigate them either, I was completely put off by the mere idea of it.

It was only when my curiosity took over that I examined the *why*s and *how*s. I quickly realized that I could fully accept and follow those rules. Some people just roll better when they have a bit more information – I guess I'm one of them! Others need to go in cold-turkey. In any case, I managed to make it through the ten-day retreat and really enjoyed the new experience.

Consciously creating habits

We need to create habits that make us change for the better. These habits will help us perform better, for ourselves and the people we love. They will help us strive to become the best version of ourselves. These habits will be uncomfortable in the beginning, but if we stay and persevere, they will 'burn' away the things that keep us from change.

This is why I also like the translation of the Sanskrit *tapas* as a 'burning passion'. Whereas *self-discipline* feels like a task that requires a good deal of effort, *burning passion* feels like something that is already there. It makes me think of success. *Self-discipline* feels like a push towards goals, but *burning passion* feels more like the goals are pulling you towards them.

Sometimes it's scary to let go of certain habits because we are so used to them, but when we do we experience significant rewards. When we are able to identify the daily habits that serve us and the ones that don't, we are well on our way to success.

> **Answer the question and act**
>
> If there is only one tiny little practical thing that you might remember from this book, I hope it will be asking yourself every day the following question: *what three things must happen today for me to move forward with my life goals?*
>
> Reflect on this question before answering emails, before checking any device. Answer the question and act. Know that you can be in charge of your life; you don't need to adopt a reactive role only. Before you start responding, you can act and be creative. When you do this for a while and make it part of your morning routine, I assure you that positive things will happen.

Happy, healthy and rich

Having a strong mindset is one of the keys to self-discipline. One of the main things that has helped me the most in my personal journey is to have a motivating home-made mantra, which has pulled me into living a healthier and happier life. I share it often on retreats and in private coaching. The mantra is: 'I am happy, healthy and rich.' It encompasses self-discipline on all three aspects of body, mind and spirit and keeps me on track with my goals. Before using the mantra, I defined what the words meant to me.

The *happy* part means that I develop a state of mind so that no matter the circumstances, I will feel calm, at ease, confident, content and happy. No external factor can mess with the good feeling that I have inside of me. And, if possible, although I realize that I have little influence over this, I would very much like for people to feel better after meeting me, however brief our meeting may have been. After every single encounter I have with a person, I make sure that I have checked the colour of their eyes. I don't stare, but I endeavour to actually look deeply at every single person.

The *healthy* part of the mantra is strongly correlated with self-discipline as it has the power to pull me out of situations that are not good for me. If something is off, I recover with the speed of light. During my childhood and teenage years, I took more medicine than one can find in a decent pharmacy. Later on in life, I went completely overboard with drinking, and I smoked and neglected my body. Knowing this, I now cherish the wonderful machine that is my body and I treat it with care. Whenever there is a malfunction, I just know I will recover. It also keeps me in tune with certain habits.

This isn't always easy, though. During my retreats in Rome, I became a serious coffee drinker. Perhaps I took the adage, 'When in Rome...' a little too far. My mantra (happy, healthy and rich) has helped bring me back from this. Though I would love to drink six cappuccinos and happily top those up with some espressos, now whenever I want to order another coffee, I pause, reflect and ask myself if a healthy person with my constitution would drink another coffee. My desire to be healthy is then big enough to simply be content with what I've already had and I refrain from ordering another one.

The third part of the mantra, *rich*, is the feeling that I want to have. I want to be able to do what I love professionally without ever feeling like doing a job. I want to take any training I'm interested in, travel the world, give back to the world and take three months off per year to study and rejuvenate. Rich, for me, has nothing to do with material possessions – but I do appreciate experiences and I love contributing. I like to be able to spend 100 euros for a lunch at the Royal Mansour in Marrakesh; as long as I do this with a person I like and we both appreciate the moment and experience, I couldn't feel wealthier. I don't do these things every week, but when I want to indulge in those kinds of adventures, I can. This is how I define being rich. Rich also requires appreciating what I have. I can be happy and content every single night, realizing that I have a bed, a house, a partner, friends and everything I can wish for. It makes gratitude come easily.

I have used this mantra for years, especially on days when I didn't really feel like any of the three.

Connection fail: you can count on me

As we know, one of the definitions of Yoga is 'union', which is what we can all strive for. When you actively work on the concept of self-discipline, you can expect transformation on the union aspect. The people around you will know that when you say you will do something, you will follow through, for example. That just makes it easier for others to trust you, and to connect. They know that you will not let them down and people who reach their goals and actually do what they said they would do can inspire others.

Side note

Without harmony in the personality, it can be difficult to focus on self-control and self-discipline. It might even create more harm than good. For a person who is severely depressed or burned-out, saying that he or she should have a happy mantra and just think positive thoughts is too much to ask. For example, in the *Hatha Yoga Pradipika*, the oldest surviving text on Yoga, there is very little said about self-control or self-discipline. Here, the starting point is the purification of the body, as we discussed in Chapter 6 on purity.

Fitting self-discipline into the bigger picture

The result of practising self-discipline is that we purify ourselves physically, mentally and emotionally. Even more so, when we are able to burn off the impurities and negative aspects of life, we are able to refine body, mind and spirit. When self-discipline is mastered, we may feel contentment (the seventh principle). And when there is a strong desire to learn, we are also practising self-inquiry (the ninth principle). And knowledge liberates us. When we practise and when we offer our practice to that someone or something greater than us, we call that *surrender*. This surrender is the tenth principle.

Change-maker: centring breaths

Set a timer to go off every 50 minutes. Every time it chimes, do this tiny little breathing exercise, taking little breaks to help you feel rejuvenated throughout your day. Regardless of what you are doing, this will help you to increase productivity.

1. Take a long, slow, gentle inhalation through your nose.
2. Follow the inhalation with a long, slow, gentle exhalation through the nose.
3. Take several normal cycles of breathing through your nose until you feel refreshed.
4. Repeat steps 1, 2 and 3 for up to five rounds.

Change-maker: happiness

'Every hour, spend ten seconds wishing someone happiness. It is transformative', suggests Matthieu Ricard, a Tibetan monk who was given the title of 'Happiest Man in the World' in the Western press due to the level of brain activity registered in a brain scan during his meditation.

Change-maker: worry away!

- Set your timer for 15 minutes.
- Now start worrying. Worry the heck out of yourself! Worry about anything and everything. Horror scenarios, *what ifs...* Keep going until the timer goes off.
- When the timer goes off, take a blank sheet of paper and write down the things you can do about your future problems. Take a good look at the things you can do right here and now. Nobody needs long to-do lists of things they 'should' do one day. Instead, write down actionable things that you can do *now*.
- Do your 'actionables' and make a schedule for all the points on your list.
- Once you have done what you can do, drop the whole thing and trust that things will work out. This might be the most important step of all. You do the work and then you trust.

When I first started my business Revealing Vajra, I had to do this exercise multiple times to stop myself from losing my mind. The financial risks that I took to fund the Yoga venues for my retreats were immense. I remember once settling the final payment for my Costa Rica retreats at a point when I had exactly zero bookings. It was the end of November and I had one month to go before the Christmas and New Year retreats. By following the steps described above, I would always come up with new ideas and things that I could still do promotion-wise. And, at a certain point, I was genuinely OK with a disaster scenario as well – the famous 'it is what it is', for experts. As you can imagine, the minute I was completely fine, not just theoretically fine but really feeling a sense of calmness with this scenario, the bookings started to come in. We were fully booked for both weeks within days.

9

SELF-INQUIRY

According to Patanjali, our next principle is crucial in order to have a *successful* practice, and thus a successful life. The Sanskrit principle *svadhyaya* leads us to the topic of self-study or self-inquiry. This principle is difficult to translate in just one or two English words, as it wouldn't reflect exactly what is meant in a yogic context. If *svad* means 'self' or 'own' and *adhyaya* translates as 'lesson', 'reading' or 'lecture', we could translate this principle as 'spiritual self-study'. However, when we translate *adhyaya* using a different root (*dyhai*), it brings us to 'meditate' or 'contemplate'.

Becoming aware of and taking the time to observe yourself, your actions, your being and the world around you is the definition that I personally prefer, as practising this can lead you to be able to be yourself in the deepest possible way in these modern times.

For the record, this is not exactly what Patanjali refers to when he mentions *svadhyaya*, as this focuses on studying one's true Self, in order to connect, to unify, with the divine consciousness – to go beyond the idea that the Self is something different than what we already are. In the rest of the *Yoga Sutras* and the commentary, however, we read that becoming aware of the Self, our actions and our Being leads us to the liberation of suffering. And that's why I'm integrating this aspect in the exploration of this principle.

All ten principles in this book, and this principle in particular, can be seen as invitations to explore our minds and ourselves, in whatever way – from a psychological, philosophical, scientific or religious way; whatever works. We can come to this conclusion because we are not ascetics and we lead lives that are very different from Patanjali's students. Bringing these principles into our daily lives is key.

The crucial elements of this principle are in learning, in the broadest sense of the word, and in meditation, because it's through meditation that we will get insight and thus the knowledge to learn from.

In Buddhist meditations, you are bound to hear the terms *shamatha* and *vipasyana* at some point. *Vipasyana* should not be confused with the ten-day silent meditation course by Mr Goenka. Here, *vipasyana* means 'insight', which can only come after we master *shamatha* or 'concentration'. It might become clearer now why in previous chapters I put so much emphasis on learning how to concentrate. When we are able to calm the mind and keep it focused on a single point of attention, it's only then that we can start exploring the rest of our mind. And then we can start our self-inquiry.

A typical sentence in Buddhist environments is that 'the only way to understand reality is to observe reality'.

And thus, the only way to understand ourselves and our minds is to observe ourselves and our minds. Herein lies a massive invitation to learn.

So let's start, and let's see if we can find out a little bit more about ourselves, our behaviour, our 'wants' and desires.

Who am I?

We identify ourselves with our name, our body, our mind, our possessions, our profession, our country, our gender, our reputation and so on, but is that really who we are? Lots of people might think that *yes, this is who I am, all of it. I am a mother, a son, a grandson, a teacher, a student, a colleague, a friend, a sister, a lover, a partner, a taxi driver, a lawyer or a doctor. I am funny, smart, pretty, loving, caring and giving. I am balanced, creative, stubborn, passionate and ambitious. I am good at football and I am a pro in maths. And at times, I am irritated, tired, happy, joyful, in love, thirsty, turned on and fun, and even all of it at the same time.* That's a lot *to be* for one person only, but will this list tell me exactly who this person is? In some form or another, this list is what we usually want to know when we meet someone for the first time, in order *to get to know them.*

We love to know more about ourselves. Just look at the success of all the personality tests. In my corporate days (and maybe some companies are still using them), personality tests or type indicators like the

Myers–Briggs Type Indicator (MBTI) were essential factors in the hiring-and-firing processes. And how many people are not fascinated by astrology and can't wait to find out what your zodiac sign is? We just love to know more about ourselves and others! Don't we? Yes, no and maybe. Do these tests and our zodiac sign tell us who we really are at the core? Or do they just describe another aspect of a person? Is it not so that these tests are a very safe way of self-exploration? After all, nothing world-shocking is going to come out of them, is it? Even more so, in most cases, they provide simply a confirmation of what you already know about yourself.

It's comforting to recognize yourself in tests, labels and explanations and we eagerly accept both the confirmation and the conclusions they offer, telling us that we're not crazy after all. Unfortunately, I think we are crazy. We are all seriously delusional. We think and worry about the reality that we see, shape and perceive in our minds, but in fact, do we even know what reality is? Patanjali tells us that our vision of reality is blurred by our fears, emotions and other factors. We also worry about the future, but keep thinking about the past. This is bizarre.

The only antidote that keeps us from becoming even more delusional is to be aware of the thoughts that don't serve us – to create some headspace, some clarity and insight in order to deal with our anxiety, stress and fast-paced daily lives. With a trained mind, you will be able to pause, reflect and choose a different stream of thought at any moment.

Me, myself and I

When I am pointing at myself, I'm pointing at the 'I'. But where is 'I' exactly located? We point at the body, maybe at the head or at the heart but, if we remember from Chapter 6 on purity, the body is just an accumulation of dirt... so, surely, that can't be all of 'me'? The question remains: who is the 'I' that has consciousness?

Who is hiding beneath all these social roles, under all these characteristics? Is it even possible to grasp this concept with our minds, as the intellectual mind is part of that consciousness and we want to look beyond? Taking it a step further: who am I when the mind is finally still and purified? When the mind is free from all thoughts, memories, beliefs, imaginations, feelings and emotions? This would be too detailed and long for the scope of this book, but this is where insight meditation starts. For now, I would like to invite you to think about it for a minute or so. What would remain of the 'I' when the mind is still and purified?

'Without food, I get hangry!', says the SPOB

Some people get hangry (hungry and angry) when they *don't get fed* on time. They just *need* food; it's hormonal, a childhood trauma or whatever other excuse they have.

For me, this is the perfect example of an untrained mind. Unless something extraordinary has happened to you in the past, if you are reading this book it's unlikely that you know what real hunger is. When you let the sense of hunger take over completely, and display anger or irritation to the outside world because you haven't had food for a couple of hours, that is a choice.

It's choosing to allow emotions to take over and that results in a behaviour. It's choosing which thoughts you are going to give your full attention. And as with any behaviour, we can choose ours.

For example, if you are hungry but all of a sudden your life is in danger, my guess is that the feeling of hunger would no longer have such a large presence. In fact, it would completely *disappear*. The reality is that you still haven't had any food but your mind is too busy tackling the potentially life-threatening danger that it doesn't have time to be a SPOiled Brat (SPOB).

You are the problem, not me

Can you think of a person who makes you feel like you're a kid? I can vividly remember one person from my corporate days. My God, that person really pushed some buttons. Whenever we met, I got catapulted straight back into feeling like an eight-year-old, in a very negative way. His overall contempt for my skills and position didn't make it any easier either. And to make things even worse, while being 30 years his junior, I was theoretically supposed to be his boss. Like I said, that was merely in theory. While I'm typing this, the smile on my face couldn't be bigger, as so many things have changed in my life. But at that time, position and function titles were a real thing, for the both of us.

When you feel like an eight-year-old, your reactions might not be the wisest, confirming to the other person the exact opposite of what you would like to bring across. The fact is that, at times, I did wonder if my position was justified, considering my lack in both knowledge and experience. Surely, my insecurity and fears weren't something that I was going to bring to the table, but when someone challenges you in that very domain, things can get tricky. He triggered me to become better at warp speed, working day and night to prove him (and lots of others) wrong, which I did. Unfortunately, for lots of people these encounters just add more work frustration, at times becoming a reason to quit.

Why did our friction not frustrate me? Because very quickly I admitted to myself that my ego needed to step aside in this matter and that I got triggered because of my own insecurity. I could start disliking him, but checking in with myself and zooming in on my part of the deal in our interaction would be much more effective.

I quickly found a way to work very well with this person and not go for easy wins any longer, nor talk behind his back (oh yes, very guilty, sorry) or ignore him altogether as I realized he really was a gift to me. He was right: there was room for improvement, on all aspects of my role in the company, so I took that lesson to heart instead of being all stubborn about it – which had been my inner eight-year-old's preferred reaction.

I hear this same story too often in my coaching conversations. 'Someone' at work is causing you a ridiculous amount of stress, pushing you into behaviours you do not want to display and the situation is making you think about leaving. If it's for this reason only, I would strongly advise you not to leave. If you don't learn how to deal with this person and heal whatever is hurting you, the chances are that in your next working environment you will run into the exact same issue. The person will look very different but the problem will be the same. We can't run from these kinds of issues; we need to learn from them and move on.

It's not just on the work floor that we run into these kinds of situations. Someone in your in-law family, your tennis club, your church, the school committee, your Yoga retreat; someone could trigger you anywhere! Find out what it is that they trigger in you and heal that aspect of your soul that's hurt. Be nice and gentle to yourself – the first principle is always there; give it time and trust that you can heal it, whatever it is.

The ego at work

Here are three simple questions that can help you snap out of an ego-driven battle: How would the best version of myself react to this situation? How will I look back on this situation in one year? What would the Dalai Lama do – or someone else who I admire for his or her kindness, compassion or wisdom?

Do you like me? I like you already!

When meeting new people, we tend to behave in mysterious ways, to say the least. Whether it's meeting someone in a romantic setting, like on a date or in general, we have developed this concept of *keeping people at a safe distance. I won't show too much of myself till I know this person a little bit better. This way, I can't get hurt; I have been hurt enough.*

The problem with this approach is that you're holding back. You're not being your authentic self, which makes most people react. The reaction will be that they will also hold back. If we're all holding back, what are we doing to each other on this planet, I wonder? We want more connection but we act like we don't care about other people. We don't let other people in and, for sure, we're not going to let other people know that we like them before we have it confirmed that they like us! And you wonder why people feel more and more lonely these days than they've ever felt before?

People often think that I'm coming on to them, the reason being that I seem to be completely open, rather vulnerable and honest. Add to the mix that I like people, that I'm a great listener, that I try my utmost not to judge and that I'm not afraid to look people in the eye, and the 'assuming' starts. The things that I consider to be completely normal behaviour in any relationship aren't so normal any more in today's society. What I do know is that I do have deeper connections with more people than ever before, and the more I live by the Yoga principles, the richer my life becomes. Rich as in having true connections with people, so many beautiful people, so I never have a feeling of loneliness, although I spend a whole lot of time by myself.

Show me the real you

I can only wish that you have the same experience, that you truly connect with lots of other people and you constantly meet new and awesome people, but for that to happen you must really open up (more) and show other people your authentic self. Unfortunately, you could get hurt again, or not. It's a chance you need to take. And, I'm afraid that not everybody will like you either, which is their mistake. For real, this should be your attitude when you meet new people. Do you like me? No? Well, I like you already. Just know that some people will never like us; whatever we do to try to convince them differently, they will not like us and that is perfectly fine, so you can stop trying. There are more than enough people on this globe to be friends with.

It's never too late

What if the relationships that you have are all based on a certain image of yourself? An image that you have projected into the world? And, what if this image gets approval from the people that you like and love? I understand that you would be very hesitant in this case to show *the real you*. Will they still like you? Will they not be disappointed to find out who you really are?

To break out of this 'thinking pattern' – as this is what it is – I ask if you have ever wondered if revealing more about yourself would possibly deepen your relationships? I ask this because maybe, just maybe, there are people out there who have sensed that you are holding back. Some brave ones will have put in the effort to get to know you better, and others simply walked away. They walked away because they might have thought that you weren't interested in them, or that you're difficult to approach, or they feared you, or thought you were a bit weird.

If you find yourself in this situation, I challenge you to show more of yourself. There is no doubt that only good will come out of that decision. Living up to a certain image, whether or not you have created this yourself, is more tiring and confusing than anything else.

Regarding the people that will be disappointed in you when they get to know you better? Let them be disappointed. Expectations are created on both sides but it's only when we are honest that something truly worthwhile can be created! Trust yourself and the others.

It's so incredibly important to reflect on what triggers us, what frightens us.

Pema Chödrön tells us the same: 'Feelings like disappointment, embarrassment, irritation, resentment, anger, jealousy and so can teach us where it is that we are holding back.' Self-inquiry can make us break free from certain habits, emotions and mental afflictions that do not serve us. That's why freedom is being considered to be the most important result of self-inquiry.

Beginner's mind

If we see everything around us as our teacher, we have an attitude of openness and curiosity. Often referred to as *having the beginner's mind*. I have taught the '10 Principles Workshop' over a 100 times by now, and it's different every single time, as I ask for interaction. There's always a different vibe, a different setting and so on. It's so amazing to notice that I still learn so much during every single workshop as people give me different angles on how they interpret certain aspects of the principles, or they see things from a different angle altogether. As Richard Bach said, 'we teach best what we most need to learn'; every single time that I teach the Yoga philosophy, I totally agree with him.

It takes courage, curiosity and openness to be able to allow the beginner's mind. New ideas may rattle your cage and this is not a nice feeling if you've tried so hard to get things in order. That's why so many people are genuinely afraid of meditation. They say: 'It took me 22 years to deal with my traumas. I don't want them to come back and haunt me again. Meditation might bring it all back.' This is true, in a way.

The fact that you're afraid that memories might resurface tells me that you haven't really dealt with them. You haven't yet found a way to look back at the past and leave it where it is. When ideas, fears or anxieties resurface in our lives, know that it's no longer the current situation. Look at it for what it is to you at that very moment: a memory. It cannot hurt you at this moment, so it's safe to look at it. From a distance. There's no need to dive back into it and get hijacked by memories and thoughts that are being burped up.

Did you know?

On another level, having the beginner's mind also refers to actual learning. What was the last thing you learnt? As in learning to speak a new language, or learning a new skill or a new sport? It's my personal ambition to learn 'something' new every single day. It can be anything.

I remember that from a very young age I would randomly pick books from the library. I would have a list of books that I wanted to read, but I always added one book that I took without looking at the cover. Today, the library has become airport bookstores, but I still do it – randomly picking out books, being incredibly surprised sometimes by the things that people actually write books about.

Why do I do the things I do?

Learning about ourselves can be extremely fun, and at the same time brutally uncomfortable, but it's the only way to start understanding ourselves and our relationships better. There's no better way than to ask questions – that's what we have been doing since we were kids. Even questioning *when* we stopped asking so many questions is interesting. Or do you still ask a lot of questions?

Below is a nice list of questions to occupy yourself with; you may add the 'why' question after every answer you give. Before you get cracking, it's important to keep the very first principle in sight when answering. If you encounter answers that you don't particularly like about yourself, be nice, be ever so nice.

Instead of potentially bringing yourself down and delivering loads of unnecessary mental comments, why not try to figure out why you do what you do? What is there that makes you act in this way? What needs healing?

- How can people hurt you?
- What was your last lie?
- Are you usually on time or late?
- What drains your energy?
- What is your most valuable item?
- Are you sloppy or orderly?
- What are you most grateful for in your life?
- Do you follow through on your goals?
- What is your *dharma*, your *ikigai*, your mission in life?
- What do you look for in a partner?

Bonus questions

- What made you pick up this book?
- What makes you continue reading?
- What makes you interested in these teachings?
- What do you hope to find here?

Connection fail: the temple of I

Remember that I mentioned in Chapter 1 that we have about 20,000 to 50,000 thoughts a day? What if I tell you that the majority of those thoughts are about ourselves? Most people are constantly questioning themselves, worrying about future or past events with themselves in a leading role. Even worrying about other people involves us, as the main idea is that 'I' am worrying. It's a temple of 'I' and 'me' and 'ego'.

- How do I look?
- What will she think of me?
- How will I do that?
- I miss him.
- I am awesome.
- How will I make it through this dinner?

One of the definitions of Yoga is 'union', which is ultimately what we all strive for – more connection with ourselves, more union with the people we love, with the people we work with, and maybe even with strangers. If we could think more of others, even for a moment, truly considering other people's needs, life might just become that little bit easier and we would instantly feel more united with others.

It might seem like a fine line to put such an emphasis on self-inquiry and at the same time talk about union with others, but it's not that fine. The self-inquiry is not done from an egocentric point of view; in fact, we do the work of knowing our true Self better for the benefit of ourselves and others. The better we know ourselves, the easier it will be to connect with others, to communicate and deal with others.

Very practically, if we know what triggers us, we can catch the frustration in the moment and be aware of it, which means we can change our thoughts and behaviour. Some sources tell us that we are suffering because *we forgot who we are*. And while this simple sentence could lead us to many different topics, why not try to show your true Self a bit more right here and now? Show more people when you are afraid, or hurt, or very happy.

We are all so happy that we are unique and not alike. I drive a black Tesla and you drive a red Fiat, in which I don't want to be found dead. I listen to hip-hop while you listen to Bach. I love hamburgers and you are on a plant-based diet. My job is all about mergers and acquisitions and you sell beer. We define ourselves with all kinds of *concepts* that are exterior to ourselves and we allow them to completely define us.

Imagine meeting someone and being able to skip all of that external stuff and instantly start connecting on another level. That is pure union. There are retreat participants who come back for the fourth time and I still don't know exactly what their job is. This is one of the reasons why on the week-long retreats I embrace the silence day so much. During that day, not only do we all speak the same language; it's also about energy and connecting on a different level.

Who we really are is difficult to put into words, but we are no different at the core. In fact, we are all the same, as we are all energy. When more people truly believe this, we can stop blaming each other and start respecting and loving each other more – or at least try to understand and support each other as we're *in it together.*

Kriya Yoga

As we saw before, all ten principles are linked, but Patanjali puts an extra emphasis on uniting the last three principles. In his *Yoga Sutras*, he refers to the last three principles as *Kriya* Yoga: what you need to become successful in your practice.

This is how he links self-discipline, self-inquiry and surrender: we need to cultivate passion and self-discipline. Even if this means that there is some kind of *pain* involved. Such as not feeling like meditating early in the morning, but doing it anyway (accepting the pain) because you know it will benefit you in the end. It will purify your mind from delusional thoughts.

The principle of self-inquiry is shown in having the desire to know your true Self; when you can embrace this knowledge as well as the teachings of *our divine teacher*, then you step into the topic of our next and last principle, of surrender.

Change-maker: soham (pronounced so-hum)

One technique to train the mind is to recite the same words over and over again. These words are referred to as *mantras*, which literally means a tool for the mind. One of these *mantras* I would love to share with you is *soham*, translated as 'I am; my true identity is'. The technique couldn't be simpler, so give it a try after reading this.

On every inhale, you mentally say 'so', and on every exhale, you mentally say 'hum'. That's it! You may practise this for 2 minutes, for 6 minutes, for 12 minutes or for two hours and everything in between. As you wish.

Every time you're getting too distracted by thoughts, you bring your attention back to *soham*. This is so incredibly effective to learn how to concentrate and to get some insight into how distracted we get. I have years and years of practice and I still enjoy the calming effect of this mantra.

There could be a world of thoughts popping up in your mind between saying the words *so* and *ham*. That's perfectly fine. There will always be thoughts – the difference is that we stop chasing after every thought. We remain calm and see or hear the thoughts, or we are aware of the thought but we don't chase after it. We remain calm and continue with our mantra. And that is when the magic starts happening.

It takes practice, a lot of practice. A person doesn't become a brilliant violinist overnight, do they? It's the same thing: practice. We need patience and kindness with ourselves, and to just do the work. If your mind wanders off and there's one thought that gets all the attention, it means that you are distracted. You're taken into memory lane, or some emotional dream scenario or *what-if* issues. You have stepped away from *what is*.

The cool thing is that at some point you realize that you have wandered off, and that is meditation in itself as well. To bring the attention back. Over and over again.

Change-maker: review your week, review your life

This is an excellent tool for self-evaluation and self-study. It's the starting point of my coaching sessions and it gives you a very precise idea of where you're at in your life. I do this review every single week to keep myself on track with the things that I find important and to hold myself accountable to my own progress.

When I see a low mark on sleep, for example, I plan in three days when I will be in bed by 10pm. When the family mark is low, I will check in with my mom, maybe send flowers. When a mark is very high, I will reflect for a minute on the things that I can do this week to keep it high.

On a scale from 1 to 10 (where 1 = nothing and 10 = I am living my dream), score the following aspects of your life.

- love
- career
- finance
- family
- friends
- spirituality
- interests, passions
- contribution
- work/life balance
- living environment
- time management
- fitness
- weight
- diet
- health, energy level, sleep
- self-discipline
- clarity of goals
- stress management
- addictions/bad habits
- motivation level
- self-confidence
- self-love
- general happiness

10

SURRENDER

We have arrived at our final principle, of surrender – *ishvara pranidhana*, with *ishvara* being the Sanskrit word for 'God', 'ultimate reality', 'true Self' or 'the divine', and *pranidhana* meaning 'to dedicate' or 'to surrender'. Literally, this principle is inviting us to *surrender to our higher Self*.

If you're instantly triggered, assuming that there's some kind of a hidden religious agenda in the principles, after all, you can relax; have no worries – there isn't. Quite a few people feel uncomfortable the minute *God* comes into the picture. They get triggered by their past, or by their present, as devotion to religion could mean many things.

The tenth principle is about surrender and trust – trust that everything will work out. So, if this principle isn't religious in the classical sense, as most of us know it, let's explore what it can mean to us in our modern lives.

This chapter also links back to the other principles, showing us how closely interlinked they all are, and it gives us an overview of what we have been exploring.

Namaste

The meaning of *namaste* is 'the divine in me sees, acknowledges and greets the divine in you'. This word is often used at the end of a Yoga class to greet each other. No, it doesn't mean 'thank you and see you all next week...' No, it's not written as *nama-stay* either; that was just a word joke in the first chapter to maybe help you remember the meaning here.

I can't think of a more beautiful thing to say to another human Being. I even said it at my grandmother's funeral to wish her a safe journey onwards. If we treat everything, every Being, with care, as if God or something divine was really inside, we would act differently. We would have more respect for other people, for all people, no matter what nationality, religion or political orientation, as these are just concepts we use to control our reality. It's not who we really are.

What does it even mean to be Dutch or American? To be Hindu or Muslim? To identify more with the Left than with the Right? We tend to identify ourselves with these concepts and ideas of who we are, but at the core, both Americans and Dutch are the same, exactly the same human Beings, with their fears, strengths and weaknesses. The only thing that separates them is where they were born. It's when we start to see how we are all alike instead of different that we can grow into the feeling of being united.

Some sources translate *ishvara* as a state of collective consciousness, which means that it represents all of us, and thus that we are united as human Beings with all other human Beings. We are so much more connected than we know. You think of someone and they send you a text message that same day – has that ever happened to you? There are many different ways of explaining this and the collective consciousness theory is one explanation. If the idea is new to you, there are quite a few studies and books about this topic; I highly recommend that you dig a little further. Just typing 'what is coincidence?' into any search engine will keep you busy for a while.

To see God in everything is something very different to religion as such. Being grateful because we have this wonderful life, because we have the opportunity to live, is divine in itself. On many occasions it can feel like a burden but, breaking everything down, the fact that you are alive right now is a gift – a divine gift.

I talked about how we always want to be special, to stand out and never fit in, but at the same time, most of us are desperately looking for union, connection and love and being special or famous is just a way to try and get exactly that. This chapter takes us a step further, as being special or standing out means absolutely nothing on a bigger plain.

What Patanjali wants us to understand is how we can connect with our true Self. Our true Self doesn't need the approval or the recognition of others. It is nice to receive, but there's no need for it.

Karma

Karma means 'action', and it's very interesting that the word *karma* is now part of the English vocabulary as well. It is interesting as in an ideal world this would mean that everyone who uses the word also understands the meaning of the word and, thus, that we would be conscious of our every action.

The word is so embedded in our culture nowadays, but unfortunately the opposite is true for the majority of human Beings. We go through the motions, we do hundreds of little actions every day and we are more mindless than ever. It seems that the more we speak of mindfulness and go on courses, the less mindful we actually become.

The goal here is to become mindful of your actions and energy, all of them, throughout the entire day. This includes your thoughts, emotions and feelings, as they are energy too.

Everything that surrounds us is an expression of who we are. This includes politics and the political regime we live in. I can't remember where I read it, but it resonated: 'we can never get a government that doesn't belong to us', which is in line with words that are very familiar to me: 'whatever matches us, comes to us, for that is law' (Esther Hicks channelling the teachings of Abraham).

This also means you will always get the relationships that suit you at a particular moment. The problem you are facing right now in your life is the very problem that you need to learn. You will not receive more, and you will not receive less, not on an individual level and not on a collective level; this is what we need right now. 'You can't always get what you want / But if you try sometimes, well, you might find / You get what you need' – the Rolling Stones, anyone?

There is no need to jump out of your seat and start screaming about free will. *Is there no free will? Is everything predetermined?* You might say that *you didn't choose to go through this mess and misery!* And if you know how a relationship break-up feels, you will say for sure that you neither wanted to feel that way nor asked for any of this. Just by formulating it the way I did, however, means that I *did* need it and that I *did* choose it. *I didn't choose this* means that you disagree with the situation, with the way life unfolds, and you don't take responsibility for it, so instead you start blaming. If you keep seeing things like you have always seen them, nothing will change.

What is free will, anyway?

You can choose to step away from habits and patterns that no longer serve you. Identifications that you have learnt in the past, which have served you for a while, you can now choose to step away from.

We are all very good at making up stories justifying why we don't pursue what we really want. We have seen them earlier in this book. Things like *Oh, I can never be thin – we are all fat in the family; we have big bones.* Or *Oh, I can never be rich – in our family, we will never have money.* These beliefs are limiting but they let you off the hook and you feel comforted by the story. Comfort on the surface, that is, as deep down you know it's not true. And it's exactly this knowledge, the fact that you know that you're making up stories, that will cause frustration and jealousy towards the people who do manifest their (your!) dreams.

Consider the following if you think that you might have some limiting beliefs that are holding you back. Stop buying your own bullshit! Stop being a SPOB! Instead, model the people who are manifesting what you want. Learn from them instead of criticizing them and start believing in abundance, as there is enough for everyone. Lots of people with a lot of cash are really cool. Choose freedom and action over the fear of failure.

Reality

The word *ishvara* can also be translated as 'ultimate reality'. The fact is that we will never be able to fully grasp reality as it is. What we have are our own perceptions, ideas, beliefs and sensory input. The things we see, hear and find to be real are just a fraction of what reality truly is.

Illustrating this perfectly is the well-known example of the car accident that is viewed by three eye-witnesses, who are all at the exact same spot, waiting for the bus. When asked, they will all have very different versions of the accident. The mother will have seen that the kid just escaped. The biker will have seen that there was a very expensive lightweight bike that got trashed, but he might have missed the kid entirely. The car lover clearly saw that a very special car had been involved in the accident and can't recall any kid.

This example shows us that we only see a very small part of reality and we make up stories for the rest – stories that we believe are true and have happened but are mostly projection, perceptions, ideas, beliefs and so on. If we want to grow, we need to stop pretending that we know reality, as what we know of reality is such a small part of it, and it's our own reality and not Reality with a capital R.

'That is just the way it is. Those are the facts'

Whenever I hear someone say something like this, I cringe; in my world, there is no such thing as *knowing everything about reality*.

It's a really great question to ask yourself: do I have all the details to judge this situation or this person?

> *All* of them? If yes, OK; go ahead and judge. If not, hold your judgement.

Trust

Surrender and trust are closely related. Trusting in the flow of life itself, for example.

A quote from Wayne Dyer in *The Shift* was that 'EGO' means 'Edging God Out'. This is best seen with parents and newborns. 'Yup, awesome, thank you God, you did very well in having this baby grow for nine months, we will take it from here.' Trusting the flow of life a little bit more is a lesson that I gladly learn and share from the concept of *ishvara pranidhana*. When you think of it, control is an illusion anyway. We think we have control but it's a total illusion. We don't have control. And the more we fight reality in trying to have control, the more it will turn against us.

We tend to think and worry ourselves crazy everyday but it becomes even more troublesome when our gut feeling tries to tell us something that our controlling mind doesn't want to accept.

If you are having doubts about a trip, or something you want to buy, or somebody you don't know if you can trust, a relationship you're about to embark on, and your intuition is trying to tell you something: please *listen*! It will save you so much time, effort and pain. Breathe, relax, release, listen and *trust*.

Surrender: release the struggle

With synonyms like 'give up', 'give in', 'crumble', 'succumb' and 'quit', the idea of surrendering is not a popular one. In a day and age when we are supposed to manifest our dreams, surrender feels like something extremely negative, to be avoided at all cost.

'Stop resisting' explains the message a whole lot better for me. When you stop resisting, you are still going full-steam ahead to reach your goals; you're not manifesting any less but you become aware when a struggle appears.

Bringing the Yoga philosophy into practice and into our daily life is all about becoming more aware. Aware of when you feel like being in a flow and aware of when the odds are seemingly 'against' you. It's about creating a harmony with the entire universe and every single person you meet, which is the ultimate result of surrender according to Patanjali.

Whatever

You can't control what people will think of you. Consequently, there is no point in trying to put up some kind of a version of yourself to please other people. Showing yourself is the central theme throughout the book, surrendering to the fact that there will be people out there who will not like you. Whatever you do to please them, they will never like you and it might not have anything to do with you.

You might look like or speak like their sister with whom they have a horrible relationship. Every time you speak or pop up, they are reminded of their painful relationship and, thus, they decide they don't like you. Is it really that simple? Are we not more evolved than that? Unfortunately not – most people simply react to what comes to them without being aware of what is really going on to cause their reaction.

Some people are more evolved and become aware of their reactions; they practise *self-study*, our previous principle. Why do we react the way we do? Someone who's familiar with the concepts that I describe in this book will notice when they are feeling off-balance. They will notice the uncomfortable feeling that comes from meeting someone. And, because they are aware, they will be able to accept and examine the feeling.

You remind me of...

In a split second, an aware person can have the following thread of thoughts when meeting someone. *How interesting, the presence of this person makes me very uncomfortable. What causes this feeling? Oh gosh, she reminds me of my sister, that's it! I have to do something about that relationship with my sister, and I will. In the meantime, right here and now, this person has nothing to do with my*

> *problems with my sister, so let me open up to her in*
> *the kindest way I can. Let me practise one possible*
> *reaction to my sister.*

Acceptance as the antidote

We need to accept the situation that we find ourselves in, in order to release the struggle, realizing that a situation is neither bad nor good, but that it simply *is*. Moreover, that it's a consequence of our own creation. It might not be the ideal situation; it could even be a very awkward one. But, acceptance brings us back to the present moment.

Accepting where we are prevents us from dreaming about a future and using it as a tool to run away from the present. The more we run away from what we don't want, the more focus and attention the present gets, the more unlikely it is things will change.

Accepting also prevents us from feeling guilty about the past. If only I had done this differently or if only I had said that, the present situation wouldn't be what it is right now. This way of thinking will probably give you more trouble than pleasure, as it will emphasize and bring into reality more of what you don't want.

Accepting where you are, being grateful for what the present is teaching you, is incredibly valuable. At that same moment, you can decide how you would like to go from here.

As we saw in Chapter 7 about contentment, we don't condemn our current situation or our current state. We accept, we are grateful for the teachings and, going forward, we might make changes. Never judging, never disapproving; instead, learning and moving forward.

Of course, this is hard when we lose our job, get sick all of a sudden or when someone breaks off a relationship and says they don't love us any more. And still, it's at the moment that we can accept what *is* that we start healing and growing.

The universe gives us exactly what we have asked for. The minute we truly accept this, our lives can change. Even if we do get ill, in many cases, the thing we have asked for for so long might have been to receive more love and attention. By getting ill, this is exactly what we got: more care, love and attention from other people. This is definitely not the case for everyone who gets ill, but for quite a few, there is some truth in this reasoning – however painful it may be to admit.

How?

Instead of thinking *why does this happen to me? Why me? I didn't ask for this! It's so unfair. I don't succeed and I work so hard*, ask the following questions.

How did I get here? What are the steps that I took to get to this point in my life? What did I (secretly) ask for? If someone would want to end up in exactly the same situation as me, what steps would they need to take? How would they need to start thinking and acting?

It's the same as we saw before with the other principles: surrendering is something very active. To surrender is an active choice, not passive at all. Active kindness is non-violence; telling your truth is non-lying etc.

Maybe – we will see

There's an old Chinese story about a farmer whose valuable horse runs away one day. All the neighbours came round that evening to say how awful it was, but the farmer replied: 'Maybe – we will see.' The next day, the horse returned and brought seven wild horses with it. All the neighbours said that it was a blessing. And the farmer said: 'Maybe – we will see.'

When the farmer's son fell off one of the wild horses the next day while trying to tame it and broke his leg, everyone felt bad for him and told him how unfortunate he was. But the farmer just said: 'Maybe – we will see.'

Soon after, the army came through and took all of the young men from the village to fight in a brutal war, but the farmer's son was spared because of the broken leg. All the villagers told the farmer how lucky he was, and he just replied: 'Maybe, we will see.'

This story shows us that really good things come from seemingly bad events, but that only time will tell us the whole story; it's impossible for us to tell if something is good or bad. The unfolding of events is of immense complexity and we just need to trust the universal law of life that, in the end, everything will work out. Having this faith allows us to surrender to divine guidance and timing. Our purpose will be revealed to us when the timing is appropriate.

Meditation

In meditation, you surrender to the silence. You stop resisting and make way for raging thoughts to come by, urging you to follow your own thought patterns to escape the very act of meditating. When training the mind to surrender, we achieve more insight, focus and peace of mind.

We need to surrender and just sit, have everything come by, like an electronic screen where things can be swiped away. Thoughts come and go, but we remain firm at our practice. We are surrendering to every thought but they are not hijacking us. We stay at the practice. In this sense, to surrender means to be very strong; it's not a weak thing to do.

Why surrender in meditation?

Because we want to create space for an inner silence that can guide us towards less worry and less anxiety. For things to happen in a more flowy kind of way. Resisting and struggling is like squeezing water in your hand; the more you want to hold on to it by squeezing, the less water you will be able to hold in your hand. Letting go of control will set us free in a way that we will experience that there is no control to begin with.

Silence in our minds, or less noise, creates space for different thought patterns and ideas to arise, instead of constantly repeating the old stories we tell ourselves, instead of the constant comparison to others and to what the norm should be. Silence allows for our intuition to talk to us, and for us to hear it, to feel it. To get to know ourselves and trust ourselves, creating space for compassion and active kindness to exist.

From Antwerp to Essaouira, from in a relationship to single, from a high-flying corporate job to no 'real job'. Or, how my journey to live in Morocco asked for more surrender and trust than I wanted to give. Five years ago, I was looking for a new venue to do my Yoga retreats. I thought it never rained in Morocco, so this would give me a beautiful long season to do retreats all year long. In retrospect, I was wrong; it does rain in Morocco. Quite a lot actually.

Anyway, I instantly found the perfect venue in Marrakesh, which left me with a couple of days off and the advice to visit a little fishermen's village, Essaouira. I hardly knew how to pronounce it, but I rented a car and drove off. I arrived, parked my car and instantly said the magical words: *Oh, I can live here!* At that same moment, I put my hand in front of my mouth as I was so surprised over what I had just said out loud. It had taken me a long time to build up my coaching practice in Antwerp, and it was finally going very well. I was teaching Yoga every day, having a great time with friends. There wasn't a sensible reason in the world for me to move, let alone to another continent, where I didn't know a living soul. But, well, it felt right.

I sold and gave away everything; three months later, I found myself in a seriously cool rooftop apartment in Essaouira, a ten-minute walk from the beach. It was on my list of things to manifest – to have a really nice place, walking distance to the beach, always good weather. But I had never thought this would be in Morocco.

I fully trusted that it would work out. I took the first apartment I saw online. There was flow and full trust. I didn't even allow any thoughts or doubts to come into my mind. No fear, no worries, no anxiety.

This is how you can make decisions. This is how I ended my 12-year relationship; this is how I quit my high-flying corporate job without having a clue what to do next and moved continents. We can do some seriously cool things when there's full trust in ourselves and in the universe.

Too many people on my retreats get all inspired and excited and want to follow my lead and quit their jobs. Besides the usual two sentences 'it's all good' *and* 'please relax your shoulders', what I probably repeat the most is: 'Do not quit your job!' If you are financially free and don't like your job, then please quit your job, what's wrong with you?

Quitting a job is easy. It might give you a bit of a rush and maybe even a feel-good moment if you don't have the best relationship with your boss. Let me tell you, though, that not being able to pay the bills the months after you quit is not so much fun. It's a full-blown disaster and very soon you'll be wondering if and how you could go back to your old job. Not everyone is set up to have their own business; passive income is a massively hyped topic where it's just a few that make a lot of money, and quitting is often not the answer to your problems.

I gave away and sold most of my stuff, but certain things I wanted to be shipped to Morocco. In a way, these things were the most valuable objects that I still had. I wrapped everything up, put it into boxes and waited for the movers to pick it all up. They collected it and asked me to come by the next week to check on the packaging – they would have to unwrap everything and repack it, as they shipped in bags instead of boxes.

The next week, I guessed everything was there (the bags were all taped up so I couldn't see what was inside…) and they gave me a ten-digit number and a vague address of an even vaguer bus company. Right at that point, I knew that I had but one choice, which was to surrender completely, as there was no way of knowing if I would ever see my stuff again.

In the end it all worked out; every single thing was there and the bus company and address weren't vague at all. Now I know that an address in Morocco can be an indication and not necessarily a street name with a number.

When I quit my job, I fully trusted myself and the universe that it would be fine. I was convinced I would find my way and have an even better life with less stress and more time to myself. The key was in surrendering and trusting. And having enough money in the bank to keep me going for a year if needed – a not-so-irrelevant detail.

When do you need to give up? Does it feel like a struggle? Or, does it feel good when you think about a specific person or situation? Is there a fear? What feeds the fear – is it the doubt of making the 'right' decision?

What always comforts me is that you can't make the 'wrong' decision, ever. You will learn something every time things don't work out. You gained experience, which you may need, or may not. No guilt, no shame. These are useless emotions, as we don't learn from them.

I love the American attitude about starting your own business: there is no such thing as failure. You tried, you gained experience and you still rock. The contrast with Belgium regarding this is striking. People seem to almost gloat when your business isn't a financial success and you decide to close it. It's perceived as a failure and people will ask about all the gory details. You're back at square one, and maybe even need to go back to your old job. It has the aura of an ultimate losing of face.

But it is absolutely not the case! Time has passed, and you have the experience and never need to think again, *what if I started my own business?*, because you have done it. It's like the old neuro-linguistic programming adagio: 'There is no such thing as failure; there is only feedback.'

Connection fail: don't be naïve

Why are we so afraid to trust other people? Because we have been hurt, people have disappointed us, and other times we had different expectations. But this is just a way of thinking, because people can't disappoint us.

If there's true love, active kindness (our first principle), people will not disappoint. We will have full trust in the goodness of others. People instantly shout out the warning that I'm being naïve – another 'bad' thing to be.

Of course, we need to have our brains switched on to protect us from possible danger, but there's no real need to be cynical, sarcastic or to only see the negative in people. This can easily become an attitude, a part of you. And, if you repeat the fact of your own cynicism long enough, you will actually start thinking that you are cynical. I have never met a cynical baby. We were not born like that. It's just a projection of our view of our own life, to see the negative and mock – usually others.

Sarcasm always hurts at least one person. I used to love it – stand-up comedy too, where a comedian would mock the physical characteristics of politicians, celebrities, even people in the audience. Nowadays, I can't stand it. Why on earth would we want to hurt other people? Because it *does hurt* – especially for people who try to convince us that they have a thick skin. When someone else makes fun of you, it hurts. And it doesn't serve a single purpose, only a short-term benefit for the one making the 'joke'.

That's why we learn from a very early age that we can't trust others. *They might make fun of us later.* We tell our children that they can't bully or make fun of other kids at school but our behaviour shows the exact opposite. We think that it's OK to make fun of a person that is 'extremely' gay, skinny, big, tall, short, pretty, handsome etc. Whatever is not seen as normal. But what is normal anyway?

And then, at a certain point, when we're evaluating our relationships, we notice that we don't trust others, not even our partners. This is completely natural! We teach our kids that they mustn't trust strangers. *Don't ever go with a stranger. Not a woman, not a man you do not know. People cannot be trusted.* This is literally what we are teaching them! Out of protection from other people.

Kids still have fearlessness (the result of truthfulness – remember Chapter 2), especially towards other people. They still have the sense of union, that we are all One.

Non-violence, being One

We are all connected by a universal principle – our very first principle in this book, *love*. Love and non-violence are a choice, a mental state. This doesn't mean that we need to like everyone or that we need to be best friends with everyone.

Universal love and active kindness means having respect towards all living beings, knowing that we are all connected, being fully aware of the union. This is not the same thing as feeling sorry for other people, as this means that you put yourself above them or that you project your pain onto them; it's none of that. True compassion is different.

I witness many upsetting situations on my travels, from extreme poverty and children living on the street to all kinds of animal abuse. A simple stroll over the big square in Marrakesh could get me in tears, watching the monkeys and snake charmers. There's not a whole lot I can do, though, while I'm walking around; I can simply wish them well and give them my loving attention. At a different moment, there may be ways to tackle this issue at a more regulated level, but when simply walking around we can only send love. As long as people go on taking photos with them, it will continue. If we stop asking, they will find something else to do. This might not be in the best interest of the current animals, as they will be left without a 'purpose', but it's the best solution for the future.

May you be well and happy

I can only encourage you to often use the phrase 'may you be well and happy' – to kids, beggars, donkeys, horses, cats, dogs. To people who look sad, who can use support…

Acknowledging their existence instead of looking away helps. It helps us to keep feeling, and to keep feeling unity with every single Being on this planet.

And even though I'm not a huge fan of spiders and mosquitoes, I will not kill them. I would rather escort them out of my house or ask them kindly to leave. Try it – yes, I know how this sounds – ask ants and mosquitoes to leave instead of spraying them; it might just help. Just ask them to leave before you spray.

Please meditate

I would like to end this book with a request: please meditate.

Life is not easy, but why make it harder by having an uncontrolled mind that's bossing you around the whole day? A mind that feels like evil in disguise, all those voices telling you what is wrong and dangerous.

Patanjali doesn't identify God as such, as mentioned before; it's more of a philosophical concept. This means that Yoga as such is not a religion. It's far more of a psychology for the mind, learning to explore the mind, getting more insight into the mind. And you can start getting more insight by observing the mind in mindfulness practices, which is the first step in meditation.

If there's only one lesson to remember from this book, make it the concept of non-violence. Non-violence as the ultimate foundation for all other principles. Some teachers tell us that the other principles, in a way, are just there to teach us about being non-violent.

The beauty of it all is that we just need to relax, release and come home. To what has always been there and will always be there. We are One; there is union with the universe, with each other – we just tend to forget this.

I won't take it too far on the spiritual side here, but the only thing most people want is to have more union (Yoga!), more connection, and the only thing that a lot of people tend to do is create more distance by not showing their true Self.

Thank you so much for reading this book. I very much enjoyed writing it and I hope you have enjoyed the exploration of the principles.

My invitation to you is to keep breathing, relax your shoulders, release, to practise and to trust; it is all going to work out.

Namaste.

GLOSSARY

This brief glossary is a guide to the Sanskrit, Pali and Traditional Chinese Medicine terms used in this book. To spell Sanskrit and Pali words in English, diacritics were excluded.

ahimsa: non-violence (Chapter 1)

anicca: the belief that all things are impermanent and constantly changing

aparigraha: non-grasping, non-possessiveness, non-clinging, non-greed, or non-attachment (Chapter 5)

asana: posture, seat; the third limb of Patanjali's eight-limbed Yoga path

ashram: a place for spiritual practice

asteya: non-stealing (Chapter 3)

atman: the inner Self, God

ayurveda: literally, the science of life; one of the Indian systems of medicine

brahmacharya: the one who lives in constant awareness of the universe (Chapter 4)

brahman: pure consciousness

Buddha: the Awakened one

dharana: concentration, binding consciousness to a single focus; the sixth limb of Patanjali's eight-limbed Yoga path

dharma: very difficult to translate in English; it's a way of viewing reality, a reason for being, a duty, a task of life

dhyana: meditation; the seventh limb of Patanjali's eight-limbed Yoga path

dyad: two units treated as one, a listening structure between two people

Hatha Pradipika: a medieval scripture, one of the oldest texts on Yoga

Hatha Yoga: literally, 'forceful yoga'; nowadays used as a generic term to address the more physical aspect of a Yoga practice

ishvara: a state of collective consciousness, ultimate reality

ishvara pranidhana: surrender to our higher Self (Chapter 10)

jala neti: a technique to cleanse the nasal passages with saltwater

jing: a term from Traditional Chinese Medicine; primal energy

karma: action; the 'laws of *karma*' refer to the laws of cause and effect

klesha: affliction, obstruction, obstacle, cause of suffering

Kriya Yoga: linking the last three principles: self-discipline, self-inquiry and surrender

Mahabharata: ancient Indian epic

mantra: literally, 'tool for the mind'; short repeated words or sayings

namaste: 'the divine in me sees, acknowledges and greets the divine in you'

niyama: internal discipline; the second limb of Patanjali's eight-limbed Yoga path (Chapters 6–10)

Pali: classical Buddhist language

panchakarma: Ayurvedic cleansing programme

Patanjali: yogi and sage who compiled the *Yoga Sutras*

Patanjali's eight-limbed Yoga path

- limb 1: *yama* (Chapters 1–5)
  - *ahimsa, satya, asteya, brahmacharya, aparigraha*
- limb 2: *niyama* (Chapters 6–10)
  - *saucha, santosha, tapas, svadhyaya, ishvara pranidhana*
- limb 3: *asana*
- limb 4: *pranayama*
- limb 5: *pratyahara*
- limb 6: *dharana*
- limb 7: *dhyana*
- limb 8: *samadhi*

prana: life force, also referred to as qi, chi and ki

pranayama: breathing techniques; the fourth limb of Patanjali's eight-limbed Yoga path

pratyahara: withdrawal of the senses from their objects, beyond the mind; the fifth limb of Patanjali's eight-limbed Yoga path

sadhu: literally, a good person; in this context, one who leads a spiritual life, a wandering monk

samadhi: a state of mind; the final limb of Patanjali's eight-limbed Yoga path

samsara: the wheel of birth and death; the flow of the world, a cycle that goes round and round endlessly

Sanskrit: the classical language of India; the language of the *Yoga Sutras*

santosha: contentment or satisfaction (Chapter 7)

sat: true essence, true nature, that which is true or even 'to be; being'

satya: truthfulness (Chapter 2)

saucha: cleanliness, purity (Chapter 6)

shamatha: literally, 'tranquility', 'serene stillness'; it also embraces a range of meditative techniques and is a state of mind

shen: a term used in Traditional Chinese Medicine to indicate the spirit, consciousness, mental wellbeing or mental vitality

soham: a popular mantra, meaning 'I am', 'my true identity is'

steya: to steal, to rob

sutra: literally, 'thread'; aphorism; condensed verse

sutra neti: a technique of nasal cavity cleaning using a cotton thread

svadhyaya: self-inquiry (Chapter 9)

tapas: heat; intensity of discipline, self-discipline (Chapter 8)

Upanishads: ancient Sanskrit texts of spiritual teaching and ideas of Hinduism

vajra: diamond; thunderbolt; a diamond has been my logo since I started organizing Yoga retreats to symbolize revealing the diamond within, the beauty within people, as I believe we all have a bright and shiny diamond within us

Vedas: a collection of scripture dating back to 1500 BCE

vipassana meditation: ten-day silent meditation course by Mr Goenka

vipasyana: literally, 'insight'; it also embraces a range of meditative techniques and is a state of mind; confusing, as it sounds similar to *vipassana* (see above)

yama: self-control, restraint; the first limb of Patanjali's eight-limbed Yoga path (Chapters 1–5)

Yoga: literally in this context, 'union'; uniting with who you've always been, your natural state of being

Yoga Sutras: 195 (196 in another version) 'threads of wisdom', written around 200 BCE by Patanjali, explaining 'Yoga'

BIBLIOGRAPHY

Adele, Deborah. *The Yamas & Niyamas: Exploring Yoga's Ethical Practice* (Duluth, MN: On-Word Bound Books LLC, 2009).

Bryant, Edwin Francis. *The Yoga Sutras of Patanjali: A New Edition, Translation, and Commentary with Insights from the Traditional Commentators* (New York: North Point Press, 2009).

Burchard, Brendon. *High Performance Habits: How Extraordinary People Become that Way* (Carlsbad, CA: Hay House, 2017).

Chödrön, Pema. *When Things Fall Apart: Heart Advice for Difficult Times* (Boulder, CO: Shambala Publications, 2016).

Cope, Stephen. *Yoga and the Quest for the True Self* (New York: Bantam Books, 1999).

Cope, Stephen. *The Wisdom of Yoga: A Seeker's Guide to Extraordinary Living* (New York: Bantam Books, 2007).

Dyer, Wayne W. *Change Your Thoughts – Change Your Life: Living the Wisdom of the Tao* (Carlsbad, CA: Hay House, 2009).

Dyer, Wayne W. 'The Shift: Ambition to Meaning Starring Dr. Wayne W. Dyer' [film] (Carlsbad, CA: Hay House, 2009).

Easwaran, Eknath. *The Bhagavad Gita* (Tomales, CA: Jaico Publishing House, 2010).

Farhi, Donna. *Bringing Yoga to Life: The Everyday Practice of Enlightened Living* (New York: HarperCollins, 2004).

Harnham Buddhist Monastery Trust. *A Dhammapada for Contemplation* (Harnham, Belsay, Northumberland: Aruna Publications, 2010).

Hicks, Esther and Jerry Hicks. *The Teachings of Abraham. Ask and It Is Given: Learning to Manifest Your Desires* (Carlsbad, CA: Hay House, 2004).

Muktibodhananda, Swami. *Hatha Yoga Pradipika* (Munger, Bihar: Yoga Publications Trust, 2012).

Powell, Seth. *Yogic Studies. Classical Yoga Philosophy and Yoga Studies Intro Course.* Online video courses.

Robbins, Anthony. *Awaken the Giant Within: Take Immediate Control of Your Mental, Emotional, Physical and Financial Destiny* (London: Simon & Schuster, 1991).

Satchidananda, Sri Swami. *The Yoga Sutras of Patanjali. Translation and Commentary by Sri Swami Satchidananda* (Buckingham, VA: Integral Yoga Publications, 2010).

Stone, Michael. *The Inner Tradition of Yoga: A Guide to Yoga Philosophy for the Contemporary Practitioner* (Boulder, CO: Shambala Publications, 2008).

Stone, Michael. *Yoga for a World Out of Balance: Teachings on Ethics and Social Action* (Boulder, CO: Shambala Publications, 2009).

Thich Nhat Hanh. *The Heart of the Buddha's Teaching* (New York: 1st Broadway Books, 1999).

Wallace, B. Alan. *Tibetan Buddhism From the Ground Up* (Somerville, MA: Wisdom Publications, 1993).

Wallace, B. Alan. *Minding Closely: The Four Applications of Mindfulness* (Ithaca, NY: Snow Lion Publications, 2011).